ALEC MILLER

Guildsman and Sculptor
in Chipping Campden

D1464789

Ja..

The Local History Press
3 Devonshire Promenade
Nottingham NG7 2DS
Tel: 0115 970 6473
Fax: 0115 942 4857
VAT No: 385 4184 28

Campden and District Historical and Archaeological Society

ISBN 0- 9511434-7-6

Printed in England by The Vale Press Ltd

This small work is affectionately dedicated

to

M.S.Smylie

Teacher at Campden Grammar School, 1931 - 35

Alec Miller, 1903

LIST OF CONTENTS

INTRODUCTION

Our Society's first publication paid tribute to a member of C.R.Ashbee's Guild of Handicraft. *A Child in Arcadia*, which appeared in 1986, was based upon the boyhood memories of H.T.Osborn, whose father was a member of the Guild. This, our second small book, tells the story of Alec Miller, another but famous Guildsman. Written by his daughter, Jane, it deals with the life and career of a sculptor and carver whose work found appreciation on both sides of the Atlantic after financial stresses had sadly killed the Guild itself.

These memories complement Harry Osborn's story. They show how the latent intellect and artistic ability of a young Scot who had left school at twelve years of age could expand under the stimulus of a man such as C.R.Ashbee. At the same time, Jane Wilgress's book provides us with a delightful insight into life in a small English country town during the first two decades of this century.

Well-liked and much respected in Campden, there are still people living in the town who can well remember the Miller family.

Examples of Alec Miller's distinctive work can be seen in the Cheltenham Art Gallery and in the Woolstapler's Hall Museum in Chipping Campden. Many of the War memorials in the district, including Campden's, were carved by him to F.L.Griggs' design. In both St. James's and St. Catharine's Churches in Campden other examples of his work can be found.

Once again the Society is grateful to Miss Sheila Wood for her skilled work in editing the book, in providing an index, and for seeing it through every stage of production.

Geoffrey Powell, Chairman
Campden and District Historical and Archaeological Society

INTRODUCTION TO SECOND EDITION

Eleven years after its first publication in 1987, I find much pleasure in welcoming, on behalf of the Society, a new and slightly revised edition of Jane Wilgress's pleasantly evocative and important tribute to her father. This has largely been made possible by Frank and Alice Johnson, and also by Allan Warmington, who, between them, have done so much in recent years for the Arts and Crafts movement in the North Cotswolds.

Although the Woolstaplers Hall Museum no longer exists, examples of Alec Miller's work may now be found in the Exhibition Room of the Guild of Handicraft Trust in the Old Silk Mill, Chipping Campden.

Geoffrey Powell, President
Campden and District Historical and Archaeological Society

THE GUILDSMAN FROM SCOTLAND

Childhood in Glasgow

The story of Campden's invasion in 1902 by assorted characters from London has been well told more than once. We know that C.R.Ashbee's Guild of Handicraft brought about one hundred and fifty newcomers, men, women and children, into the quiet, rural community - newcomers (among whom were those with reservations about this move) who were an unknown quantity and who were looked on with suspicion by some of Campden's inhabitants. To add to the very understandable mutual distrust, Cockney speech was outlandishly incomprehensible to Gloucestershire ears, and Campden speech equally so to these invaders from London.

A further, and surely pleasant, variation was added to this encounter of accents by a young Guildsman of twenty-three who arrived alone by train, not from London but from the West, and who walked from the station to the Guild shops in Sheep Street carrying two bags, one containing carving tools. This was my father, Alec Miller, who had then and kept all his life the soft and friendly speech of the lowland Scot.

Alec Miller had been born in Glasgow in 1879, the third of seven children. His father was a cabinet-maker, and the family had lived on the third floor of a 'close' at 89 Shamrock Street. Alec has left a description of the conditions of his childhood. It was bleak enough, and strictly within the confines of the dissenting tradition, but quite evidently whatever strictures and deprivations prevailed, goodwill and affection were not lacking in the Miller family. Years later my father was to write "Looking back now it seems that if I visited Shamrock Street and Thistle Street corner today it would look as if any decently human and cultivated life were quite impossible [there] and yet I am sure it was not so in the 1880s. There were conventions, decencies, and

1

even the things of the spirit were not absent. Living close to neighbours - far too close - of course there was tittle-tattle and everybody's business was discussed and known. But on the whole it did not seem, even to a sensitive boy, to be a bad or hard life, in spite of poverty or something near it: not a poverty that left us unfed, but a poverty demanding constant vigilance on the part of mother to make ends meet."

The strictures of the Sunday observance seem to have been one of the biggest burdens on the young ones. Another tribulation was the milk round. The three eldest boys delivered milk in the very early morning before school, carrying, my father wrote, "six or seven cans in each hand", the correct can having to be handed to each customer and then carried back empty to the dairyman. The job was especially difficult in winter, working with frozen fingers in the dark and climbing up and down many slippery stairs - all for one shilling a week and a pint of milk a day.

I know that my grandfather Miller was a superb cabinet maker. A large oak gate-leg table of his making is in my home now, and I remember well a handsome oak chest and other items from my childhood. He was, though, something of an invalid, incapacitated periodically by bouts of what was then called 'biliousness' (I think it may have been migraine); he was thus not fitted to be an employee, but was able to support his family from his own shop, training his eldest son, Will, in the same profession and passing his skills on to other children also - perhaps especially to Alec, the third son. My grandmother - the only grandparent I ever knew - surely had skills too. Caring for her family under challenging conditions, she raised six of seven children to successful adulthood. She was industrious, capable - and strict. In later years she opposed quite bitterly (so I learned from a relative) her eldest son's marriage, and only tolerated those of the younger sons. All four did marry, but the daughters did not. I think Grannie rejoiced in her grandchildren, though she saw only three of my uncle Will's four children, for he emigrated with his family to Australia in 1909.

Alec left school at age twelve, having completed the sixth standard. "At school" he wrote "I was quite happy. I was active enough to be fairly good at games and I was just enough of a student to scrape through my lessons. My besetting sin was that I was incorrigibly talkative, and I hardly remember a school day on which I was not punished (with a leather strap on the hands) for talking. But I have no unhappy memories.....I don't know how much our school fees were - probably very small but yet sometimes our fees couldn't be paid and we took written apologies till such time as they were forthcoming. I'm sure they were always paid - though ironically just as I was leaving school in 1891 all fees were abolished and elementary education became wholly free". In the fourth standard he records having been hit on the head by a teacher with the heavy end of a pointer, and his mother writing a note of protest. He also records "an awakening consciousness of personal qualities and physical beauty. I was also becoming conscious of social differences, and I looked at the girls in the class and decided on one as being beautiful......In the next standard the teacher found me showing a drawing of a horse's head (copied from *Chatterbox*) to another boy. He swooped down on this - but instead of punishing me, as I expected, he asked me if he could keep it!".

My father describes Saturdays, when "The milk round being done, we boys were free and could always go to father's shop and find some outlet for our energies. Father even helped us to make and then fly kites in Passil or Kelvingrove Park or would take us to a pond where we learned to row a small boat; or we could go to concerts or dramatic readings in St. Andrews Hall and have two hours' entertainment for a penny. We saw there a performance of Burns' "Jolly Beggars" and were spellbound by the wild costumes....we were thrilled by a Mr. Harrower reciting *Tam o'Shanter*".

Sundays are described with pain. "As I look back on the restrictions and prohibitions of those Sundays in the '80s I am glad these days are past". The day meant drawn blinds, a long morning walk to church and back for the whole family (tramcars were forbidden on the Sabbath), another in the afternoon and still another to Sunday school for the older children. There could be no recreation and no reading except *Pilgrim's Progress* and Sunday school magazines. Evening brought still more Bible study and finally family prayers. About this my father is not so critical: "Mrs. Meynell refers in her life of Ruskin to this bible reading as 'an incredible humiliation' but I'm sure it was not so....Father and Mother sat at the table with the big Bible and each read two or three verses. We older ones who could read also had our Bibles and each in turn read several verses till we had jointly read perhaps three or four chapters. In this way we read the whole Bible from Genesis to Revelation at least three or four times and nothing was omitted....After the reading we all knelt at our chairs. Father and Mother prayed extempore at some length. Then we three boys each repeated the Lord's Prayer and the youngest ones a simple formula....the whole must have lasted at least an hour. After that, Mother went to a chest of drawers and from that distributed to each the clean shirts, underclothes and handkerchiefs required for the coming week".

One of the most poignant passages in these notes of my father's tells briefly of a family funeral - that of baby Matthew about 1886: "My main recollection of the funeral is going in a cab with my two elder brothers and with Father who had the little coffin on his knees. The cab journey seemed long - it was to the Eastern necropolis out on Gallowgate. I don't remember if there was any service at the grave. I know the cab was dismissed and we returned in a tramcar".

My father describes the one- and sometimes two- week holidays the Miller family took annually in July, sometimes at East Kilbride or Eagleton, later in their mother's native Ayrshire. "On these holidays" he says "I was often sketching and even trying to draw people. Drawing and reading occupied all my spare time, though play was not omitted. My landscape drawing was very childish........yet I was sure that whatever was to be my work it was to be something involving drawing".

How right he was. In the spring of 1891, a Miss Anstruther who had a studio for teaching woodcarving and who often brought work to William Miller's cabinet shop, proposed that this boy come as apprentice to her when he had completed his schooling. And so, in October of that year, at age twelve and a half years, Alec Miller found himself 'bound' for seven years, starting at a weekly wage of 4/- to serve Miss Anstruther and to learn from her. He was, he says, "radiantly happy to be in a studio atmosphere". Of his first week's wages he records that his mother put aside a florin in a top drawer and kept it there, despite frequent need of it, for many years.

Miss C.P.Anstruther, daughter of a knighted member of the Indian Civil Service, had studied woodcarving in London at the Royal College of Art. She had come to Glasgow to show her work at the big Exhibition of 1888, and had then settled in the city and opened a studio to teach woodcarving and also to execute commissions. About six months after she had taken on this new young apprentice, Miss Anstruther married one Duncan Mackay of Plockton. The marriage seems to have caused some stir, especially in the circle to which both belonged - those who had taken up the 'cause' of the crofter and the folklore and language of the Highlands.

Mrs. Mackay's pupils were mostly female. Classes ran from 10 in the morning until 4, though the apprentice worked a nine-hour day. Some of his work was simply sweeping and tidying and being an errand-boy, but he also quickly learned to stain wood and to polish it and to sharpen tools. Within three months he was assigned the simple sinking of backgrounds and since he showed some drawing skill was set to the task of tracing designs on wood for the adult carving students. All this before the age of thirteen! "Quite early", says Alec "I had to learn - and did learn very thoroughly - to sharpen tools........Pupils were expected to learn to sharpen their own but this could be avoided by payment of twopence per tool and threepence for a v tool or a veiner. I must often have thus earned my week's wages of four shillings in a busy day! The woodcarving craze was 'on the town'. A dozen years later it was all inimitably described in *Kipps* by that very observant young man, H.G.Wells".

My father could put an edge fit for a surgeon on any tool. A lifetime later than this apprenticeship era, my family's own ill-treated set of carpenter's chisels often received his attention, their indifferent quality being almost supernaturally enhanced by his expertise. Most of the many and varied tools which he acquired, both for wood and stone carving, in his very long working life were of German manufacture, which he considered the best.

How vital was this comprehensive apprenticeship to Alec Miller's development and achievement as an artist! To have mastered so many basic skills as a youngster meant that when in later years he embarked on a statue or a portrait he needed to think little about *how* the end result

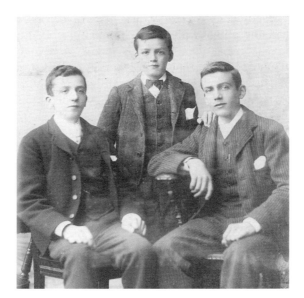

The eldest Miller Children c. 1889 L to R Jim, Alec, Will

The Miller Family 1900
Standing L to R. - Will, Cissie, Fred, Jim, Alec
Seated L to R. - Mary Curle (Granny), Bessie, William

was to be achieved: technique became, as it were, second nature - part of his being, having grown with him.

Alec remembered being sent to Edinburgh to deliver some carved work at age fourteen, his first train journey alone. By that age he was, he says, "becoming useful at very elementary bench work: and Mrs. Mackay was helping me in more ways than just carving - half unconsciously I was, I think, learning better manners, and perhaps better speech (though in our house the badly slurred Glasgow accent was not heard)". Around this age he and his eldest brother Will joined an evening drawing class. Two years later he received certificates for drawing, shading, geometry and perspective. The two brothers next joined evening woodcarving classes for boys, conducted by the Kyrle Society. The aim of this quite old-established organisation was to "keep boys off the streets" and introduce music and crafts into their lives. Alec and Will carved small objects - frames, brackets, teapot stands or breadboards. The boys paid one penny a week each, and could be supplied with wood and tools though these two brought their own. Twice a year a sale of work was held and my father mentions that while the average boy's 'take' from the sale was under 10/- he in his second year realised 30/- "because I could work faster". After the sale, some kind of social was held, with plenty to eat and then music and entertainment by Kyrle Society men and women - all of which was something of an eye-opener and what today might be called a 'mind expander' to the boys: "the first time I was ever close to people in evening dress" says my father's account.

In 1896 Alec became a student in evening art classes at Glasgow High School under Mr. William Paddock and it was here, I think, that the young apprentice became young artist. Paddock started a life-drawing class on Saturday afternoons in which he included this obviously very promising student, and a short while later invited him to join an advanced evening class which was also attended by Muirhead Bone. So the boy was doing eight hours of drawing a week in addition to a 50-hour work week at the studio - "and loved it all". In this same year Alec's younger brother Fred joined Mrs. Mackay's studio, and a carved cabinet executed by Alec was sent by Mrs. Mackay to an Arts and Crafts Society exhibition.

By 1897, having completed over five years of apprenticeship, my father felt, he says, "fairly competent". He records that he found even repetitive work had a value in teaching him more direct methods. "One job" he says "was carving acanthus foliage on more than a hundred pitchpine stair balusters. The leafage was at the top and bottom, and the length of the baluster was spiralled. The first one took me a whole nine-hour day, but I found that by working to a formula I could cut down time and after a few days I was doing three balusters a day. I believe the house and staircase still survive at East Grinstead in Surrey". Another repetitive assignment was carving 'spinning stools'. Mrs. Mackay had found the original traditional design in Fife, and these were made for sale stock in the studio. The seat was carved, and from it rose a high narrow one-piece back which was also carved with a Jacobean interlacing pattern. Alec could carve one in two hours.

Other work produced that year was the carving of panels set in a book case and a cabinet, both of which had been made by Alec's father to Mrs. Mackay's design. These panels are in low relief and represent quite elaborate scenes, with figures and animal and tree forms - an extraordinary achievement for one not yet twenty.

In 1898 Alec was promoted to journeyman status, and was paid accordingly the great sum of 30/- a week. Also that year, with Mrs. Mackay's blessing, he visited London and was taken to call at the studio of G.F.Watts. Although the great man was away, his work made an enormous impression on the young student and he records being especially fascinated by the technique and materials used in the monumental statue, 'Physical Energy'. The whole experience of London pointed up to Alec how little he knew of history and how little able he was to relate scraps of knowledge to other scraps. "Books were fairly common in our house" he writes "as compared with the houses of my companions, but guidance on the wide sea of English literature was greatly needed by a youth whose school education had ended before the age of 13. Yet the practice of the craft in which I worked was itself an educational process. The study of drawing involved some study of the lives of great artists, and sculpture could not be understood without some knowledge of Egyptian, Greek, Roman and medieval history and in my feeble way I searched for this in many books". He records indebtedness to Frederic Harrison's *The Choice of Books*, loaned to him by an uncle, and to the writings of Ruskin and Morris - although much of this material was beyond his comprehension. Through this reading, though, he came to believe that the Pre-Raphaelite Brotherhood stood for "a new imaginative life in which art and history were coherent and united". This vision he retained throughout his life, and it was, I think, through this concept of coherence that the young journeyman began to glimpse the meaning of mastery.

For three summers, at the behest of Mrs. Mackay, Alec MIller conducted woodcarving classes in Oban, an assignment which took him away from home life and his very tightly knit family. In Oban he bought books, one of them being a special number of *The Studio* containing the illustrated libretto of *The Masque of Beauty's Awakening* printed by the Essex House Press under C.R.Ashbee. The work of this dynamic architect and designer had been of much interest both to Mrs. Mackay and to her young *protégé*. They had read together Ashbee's *Chapters in Workshop Reconstruction*. In 1902, after preliminary correspondence between Mrs. Mackay and Mr. Ashbee, Alec went again to London and was introduced to the Guild of Handicraft and to its creator. The introduction led to an offer of work, though since the entire Guild was about to move base from London to Campden, enrolment was to be postponed until this move was accomplished. So my father returned to his home for a last brief time. Then came the letter notifying him that a workshop was ready for him in Campden, that he was to create and have charge of the woodcarving and modelling division of the Guild's work, and that he would have an assistant. So he sailed, on a ship of "incredibly small tonnage", from 'the Tail of the Bank' to Belfast and Dublin and finally to Bristol, and came thence by train via Honeybourne to Campden, bringing high hopes for the new employment and bringing also the Scots tenacity which was to create for him a life inseparable from craftsmanship.

THE YOUNG GUILDSMAN IN CHIPPING CAMPDEN

There are many cars on Campden High Street today, the population has increased and visitors abound - but even so the timeless and extraordinarily contained beauty of the place matches or should I say enhances the breathtaking beauty of the landscape setting. If this loveliness, overlaid as it is, can make one catch one's breath today, how much more intensely at the quiet turn of this century it must have assailed this young man from the North. Indeed, he describes his first sight of the High Street as an enchantment: "I walked up Campden's one long street entranced and happy - a mile-long street with hardly a mean house, and with many of great beauty and richness. It was, after Glasgow and Scotch village architecture, as foreign as Cathay and as romantic as the architecture of fairy-tale illustrations. In a word, it all seemed unbelievable! Was I in the twentieth century or the sixteenth? I was almost wholly ignorant of the history of architecture and building: I could not 'read' the history embodied in these stone-built houses, so rich, so substantial and of such beautiful stone. I simply walked on and on, in an ecstasy of pleasure with no thought, but just wonder. I had known nothing of the kind of place or life into which I was entering, for the glimpse I had had of Essex House in Mile End had been brief and broken (already the move to Campden had begun when I went there) and the names of Campden or Cotswolds meant nothing to a city-bred Scots youth. And yet here was Campden: I was walking up its only street and it was stranger than Paradise and more foreign!".

It was to be Alec's home for thirty-seven years.

Alec found his way to Sheep Street and the Guild shops, met the foreman and met also Will Hart, who was to work with him. Later in the day he found lodgings with a Mrs. Sargent in the High Street, to whom he paid 16/- a week for a few weeks, until he joined the group of a dozen or so Guildsmen who were to be lodged at Braithwaite House, near the Lygon Arms.

My father's beginning wage at the Guild was eightpence halfpenny an hour, with a working week of 48 to 50 hours. The first work he executed was a clock case for the library at Madresfield Court, home of Lord Beauchamp, and this was completed with such speed that W.J.Osborn, the Guild manager, recommended a higher wage for the young carver - but it is not clear whether he in fact received such a raise. (Photographs also survive of six relief panels, done two or three years later, for doors at Madresfield Court, and also of tall panels for bookcases for the library. These, as Alan Crawford[1] points out in his splendid book on Ashbee, demonstrate how particularly happy was the combination of Ashbee as designer in woodwork and Miller as carver thereof. The workmanship is sensitively in rapport with the designs, which assert alike depth of insight and whimsy.)

I think that in Alec Miller Ashbee found the craftsman of his dream. Where some Guild workers were simply "out to earn a living" as Harry Osborn[2] puts it, Alec was clearly out for learning besides earning, for life and beauty and aesthetic development. He made a whole-hearted response to the widening horizon presented to him by Ashbee, and this would surely have been gratifying to the older man. Obviously, it was a happy time. In his reminiscences of his Guild years written in the 1950s my father writes glowingly and yet with a certain awed subservience about C.R.A. (and about Janet Ashbee with unreserved admiration), but letters written between 1908 and 1911 show that he did not always feel that glow. The necessity, or the trend, in later years, to reckon with Ashbee's homosexuality and what this factor may have meant in the very existence of the Guild was, I think, something for which my father was simply not equipped. Be that as it may, and whatever was at work at the time, the encounter with Ashbee and participation in the life of the Guild was undoubtedly the second great formative force for the younger man. He brought to Campden his disciplined capacity for work and his own inherent taste for art, poetry and learning: the Guild life added, besides work, participation in drama, intellectual exchange, camaraderie, sports and fun. Such a total would lead, inevitably, to falling in love with someone, somehow, somewhere. Ashbee must have wondered.

"There was presently opened to me in the Guild an entrancing and wholly new kind of life, in which it is now difficult to separate the various elements - the new and romantic beauty of the Cotswolds, the absorbing interest of work, the widening intellectual life into which we of the Guild were introduced, the sense that we were a group enthused by a common aim and directed by one who though in complete authority over our working days was yet approachable and with whom it was easy to be on friendly and even affectionate terms". So Alec Miller, innocently and accurately, summarised the generalities of being a Guildsman under Ashbee. More particularly, he also wrote about the tremendous education it was to him to become acquainted in the Guild context with crafts other than his own: "I had known only two kinds of workshop" he writes " - my father's small cabinet shop and the woodcarving shop where I had spent the first ten years of my working life; but [at the Guild] were half a dozen other and quite strangely different craft shops, where men did strange things with iron and brass and copper, with silver and gold and precious stones. One saw men printing books...and the bookbinders stitching, 'skiving' pigskin or morocco leather.....metalworkers raising silver from a flat sheet into a saucer, then to a bowl....enamellers under whose hands the powdered glass was distributed on the copper and silver base, then fired until it fused into beautiful and permanent coloured designs....blacksmiths (whose craft I knew only as the making of horseshoes!) were to be seen forging and bending the red-hot ductile rods into beautiful curves....and the strange thing was that watching these new crafts gave one a new and deeper insight and interest in one's own craft and made one realise its potentialities. In a very real sense these experiences were educative and this education in other technical processes was such as no other workshop could provide - for no other workshop since the Middle Ages had such a diversity of craftsmen all working under one roof, with ready and open access between shops".

This unified focus of diverse skills was indeed the great appeal of the Guild concept and also its great strength. These qualities are pointed up in this description of the creative and co-operative process: "C.R.A. was commissioned to design a large silver altar cross[3] for Litchfield [*sic*] cathedral.....[he made].....the full size design on grey paper with ink and wash, using chinese white for details and highlights. The cross was to be over four feet high with a very richly elaborate base.....The cross was foliated at the ends and elaborately moulded in section: the encircling nimbus was a wheeling circle of angels in flight, repousséd in high relief and with enamelled wings. The pierced rays which supported the angels were alternately straight and waved, and these not only helped the structure but also steadied the whole design.......C.R.A. and W.A.White (the metalwork foreman) would discuss the various technical points about the design and decide to whom the work should be entrusted. The wood cross, basic support for the silver, would be given to Pyment to make.....the raising of the baroque base would be done by the most skilled hammerer of the metal shop, the repoussé......by the 'chasers', who would also pierce and repoussé the angels, after which the enamellers would fuse the colour on the wings. Meanwhile the other silversmiths would be making the cross over Pyment's wood basis, the wires and mouldings being drawn through drawplates and then soldered into position. The top end of the cross contained a recessed niche for a figure of St. Chad, first Bishop of Litchfield. I was given the job of making a model for this figure and in this way had my first lesson in the shapes and the history of clerical vestments. The figure was modelled in hard wax, then cast in plaster and finished as highly as possible in detail, and finally cast in silver and finished by chasing and engraving. When all these parts were completed the whole cross was assembled and polished......With that particular work there was quite a general celebration when it was completed and indeed it is a handsome cross and is, I trust, still on the high altar at Litchfield."

This "first lesson in the shapes and history of clerical vestments" was the beginning of much detailed research. Faced so often with work for churches, my father accumulated over the years a whole carefully annotated body of information on many aspects of ecclesiology and rubrics. In later years he could tell you the symbol or symbols of every saint - and probably the date when the symbol was first used in the history of sculpture, along with reference to examples in obscure corners of England or the continent. In 1906 he mentions another 'lesson' learned: on the back of a photograph of a kneeling angel with chalice carved for the chapel at Midhurst Sanatorium, Horsham, Alec has written "I hadn't been enlightened by the Revd. Pinchard as to holding a chalice when I did this!" All this was a very curious and surely demanding evolution of knowledge for one brought up in the utterly unadorned sabbatarianism of the Scots dissenting tradition. Furthermore, letters to the girl he was to marry make it clear that though my father was securely at home in the ungainsayable values of humanism, to him no creed touching on the divine, nor perhaps even the concept of a creed, seemed right.

Another development that must have been a challenge to the young Scot was participation in the Guild's plays under Ashbee's direction. Such an activity would have been something entirely new to Alec Miller, though I am sure his reading, already amazingly wide, would have included Shakespeare (and he had as a child gone to St. Andrews Hall for 'two hours entertainment for a penny'!). My father took to the stage with gusto and sensitivity. Good-looking and spirited, and with an unfailing memory so that he had no difficulty in learning parts, he was a stage natural, though his Scots accent gave some trouble - as did the Cockney speech of some of his fellow players. He recounts with relish the tremendous fun the participants had in these productions, and I believe he was cast in every one of the Guild plays from 1902 to 1911. Whether he ever wrote home to his parents about such activity I do not know: I expect it would have seemed sinful to them. Certainly the Miller household was not as extreme as that described by Edmund Gosse in *Father and Son*, but it is evident that my grandparents subjected their children - and themselves - to considerable stricture in the name of faith.

One participant in the play *The Fair Maid of the West*, given in the year 1911, was a girl called Olivia Rolfe. A daughter of American professor W.M.Rolfe, a friend of Ashbee's, she was destined decades later to bring tremendous changes into the lives of the Miller family - as was the young Californian geologist, Harry Johnson, whose intense courting of Olivia had brought him to Campden where the Rolfe family were spending part of a sabbatical year. He was bound to follow Olivia, and the two were eventually married. Another actress in that same play - the Guild always had to look for outsiders to play the women's parts - was Maude Royden, who also became a very special friend to the Millers, as I will show.

Braithwaite House, established by Ashbee as lodging-house for the single Guildsmen, had as overseer Will Hart, who was also Alec's assistant in the woodcarving shop and with whom he became, he later wrote, 'friends for sixty years'. Known as 'The Skipper' since he had been in the Navy, Will was popular with the young men. There was also a resident housekeeper, and a cleaning woman. The men paid 15/- a week each for room and board, made their own beds "rather sketchily" says my father, and were "plentifully but not richly fed". The one item not included in the 15/- was washing, and by the time this was covered out of a total wage of perhaps 30/- there was certainly no large amount left for spending or saving. Nevertheless, Alec Miller got himself in 1903 to Aberdeen for his brother Will's wedding, and several times while still a Guild employee he went home to share a holiday with his family in Scotland.

One Guildsman found life at Braithwaite House intolerably noisy and moved out to quieter lodgings on his own. One Londoner was so homesick that he went down to the station every day just to see the evening train arrive and depart and thus reassure himself that it would be possible to leave Campden for the metropolis. In general, life at Braithwaite House seems to have been anything but dull, and constant visitors added to the ferment and interest, for the Ashbees used space in the house for their own overflow guests. In this way the craftsmen met John Masefield, William Strang, Jack London, Walter Crane and many other interesting people. Laurence Housman was a frequent visitor, and became a lifelong friend to Alec Miller. There is a story (told elsewhere,[4] but I cannot resist telling it again) of the visitor Cecil Brewer[5] who on retiring for the night put his shoes outside his door to be cleaned. This caused consternation among the young Guildsmen, who knew they were not servants to their guests. Some had the goodwill to offer to clean the shoes, and one or two thought the daily woman could do the chore in the early morning while others were opposed to this. Will Hart held his peace while discussion raged until finally an egalitarian solution was arrived at: they put a tin of polish in the shoes and left them where they were - a gesture which was taken in very good part by Brewer.

Another visitor raised another kind of problem in hospitality. This was an engineer who had come to Campden to oversee the installation of a power saw to be housed in the lumber shed behind the Guild building. He sat down to tea at Braithwaite House and obviously unhappy at the plain fare asked pointedly if there were hotels in Campden. Receiving an affirmative answer from the men, the guest went the rounds, only to return to Braithwaite for supper since he had found the hotels to be full. His disgust was offensively evident, and the young Guildsmen began to feel hostile. They waited a while after their victim had gone to bed, then mounted the stairs carrying two sacks of empty beer bottles. Snatches of realistic drunken song and loud altercations were heard on the landing, and all the bottles were set rolling down the stairs with great effect. Next day the desperate engineer found other accommodation for the remainder of his stay in Campden.

Bicycles played a big part in the lives of workers in Campden: most Guildsmen had them and this gave them freedom to go afield in the Cotswolds or down off the escarpment to Evesham or Stratford or beyond. Alec Miller, who as apprentice and student had done much bicycling in Scotland, was on wheels almost immediately in Campden. Up until the outbreak of war in 1914, he rode regularly once a week to Shipston-on-Stour to teach two drawing classes. He arrived in time for an evening session, stayed overnight and taught a morning class before riding home (this was after the Guild had disbanded). He was still using his bicycle in the 1930s to go back and forth between home and workshop, but I do not think he ever acquired one in the United States.

ALEC & ELEANOR: COURTSHIP AND MARRIAGE

At just what date Alec met Eleanor Bishop, whom he was to marry in 1909, is not known to me. She was a sister of Gerald Bishop, a Guild director, who in the early 1900s was caught up with Janet Ashbee in an intense love affair, both of them being tried in a fire of passion and divided loyalties. While the elder brother was thus suffering, his younger sister Eleanor was more quietly capturing Alec's heart. In 1904, starting at about age 18, she had taken a post as 'mother's helper' to the family of the Reverend Muriel Nason, rector of Saintbury where the Ashbees frequently went to church since they found themselves at odds with Campden's vicar. The then childless Ashbees and the Nasons with many children (eight, if my memory is correct) became firm friends, and it may be that Eleanor got this job through her brother's connection with the Ashbees. However, some Bishop family letters suggest that the Bishop parents may also have known the Nason family.

When Ashbees took to visiting Nasons, Guildsmen also visited, and thus I believe Saintbury Rectory was in all likelihood the setting for the meeting between Alec and Eleanor. Whether either or both of them were present at the baptism of Kitty Nason in 1905 which, as has been related elsewhere [6], was to prove such a profoundly emotional day for Janet Ashbee and Gerald Bishop, I do not know.

By September 1905 Alec and Eleanor were corresponding and exchanging books and ideas. In a letter from Eleanor to Alec in that month, accompanying the return of Stevenson's *Across the Plains*, she writes: "You will notice that this is a new copy, but yours got damaged when travelling with me........I have learned wisdom - *I will never* take a book to read again on a journey with 7 children!!! I wonder if you would lend me *The Soul of a People* again, as I want a brother to read it?".

Guild Play, "The Fair Maid of the West", 1911. Standing L to R - Philipson, Alec Miller, George Chettle, Michael Pippet, Arthur Pyment, Wentworth Huyshe. Centre - Olivia Rolfe, Maude Royden, Philip Mairet. Front - Ren Huyshe, Nettie Huyshe, Charlie Downer.

Alec Miller outside the School of Arts & Crafts, c.1905

Eleanor Rowsell Bishop, 1909. She is wearing a brooch made by William Mark, given to her by Alec Miller

In 1906, Alec writes about a happy holiday spent in Scotland, yet also expresses his thankfulness at getting back to "this blessed haven of Braithwaite House". He ends this letter: "I'm going over to Saintbury tonight to try the strawberries" These two evidently shared a taste for Stevenson and for Meredith, and also for Laurence Housman's books: these authors, among others, are mentioned frequently in their letters.

My father, it is clear, fell very deeply in love, bringing to his cause all his high-mindedness and heartfelt aspirations. I am sure that my mother-to-be's feelings were in depth also, for she was a deep person, yet I believe that these feelings were not so much focussed as diffused. What comes across in the few letters of hers that have survived is her real trust in Alec. The letters are written emphasising the recurring theme of friendship: "You are my friend" is her constant statement to Alec. In late 1906 Eleanor went with one of her sisters to New Zealand and was gone many months, leaving an uncertain implication that she might not return. Letters from this long separation period suggest that Alec had to make great effort to maintain an equilibrium 'sans peur et sans reproche'. He won her in the end, but it is evident that the long uncertainty was a real trial.

Throughout this time of love and suspense, Alec was, of course, carving, earning and learning. Of particular interest, I think, is the following letter written in August 1907 when he was embarked on an enormous amount of work for the church at Calne in Wiltshire. Some of this work was designed by Ashbee but some was both designed and carved by Alec: "I told you I had to do a seated Madonna and child, and a group of the adoration of the Magi. Well the day after writing to you last I made my rough sketches. Final, I thought them then as far as composition and so on but they haven't worn well. And now I'm anxious to destroy these and do two others entirely new. I have got a little tired of the very quality which I was proud of having in my sketch for the Madonna - 'charm'. There is only one quality in art which will wear well and always give pleasure without wearying one, and that is dignity. Simple and severe it may be but still it must have that - and my little mother was graceful and dainty rather than fine......so you see today I have been steeping myself in the work of the older & earlier masters, & now I'm working to get that particular quality of distinction, & leave all the fripperies of graceful poses, pretty foreshortening & all the bag of tricks of the late Renaissance people and trying to get the simple effects of the earlier men.......I am much troubled just now over this awful problem of the relation of one's art or work to one's daily life & one's belief. A well-known architect who liked some of my work came to the Guild & enquired about carving a big screen with about 10 or 12 figures of saints. 'But' he said 'I don't think these things can be done in the real spirit except by one who is actually in close touch with the religion of the church & in sympathy with its creeds'. Well after a bit it really almost amounted to this, that our chances of getting the work were much better if the management could vouch for my religious beliefs as I wouldn't for myself! Conceive the position: I would like to get the work, but if it's conditional on subscribing to the Apostles' or any other creed I can't do it - neither for the Guild nor for the architect! I wonder if it really does affect one's work........What does it all mean? I can make little of the question - I can't believe (in the church use of the word belief) in the things I am spending so much time carving, and yet I think I can do the work as well as many people who do believe? But this is rather dull talk. I'm glad you're reading *Feverel*. What a book it is - tragedy as fine as Macbeth or Hamlet......We had our swimming sports yesterday.....I wasn't swimming as there were plenty of entries but I played on Friday in a polo match and I don't forget sports even amid the troubles of ecclesiastics and art! My three Kings call me to go on with the design of their gorgeous dress - as I get no peace at the shop I'm forced to do so on a day like this: I've escaped from Braithwaite and am writing this in Fred Griggs'[7] studio........it's delightful & quiet & I can get on.....no-one in the street - this window wide open & Campden looking very very beautiful - & me scribbling nonsense! It will let you know that I'm still here and still the same........"

That letter went to New Zealand, as did the following in September, 1907:

"I must say a little about business! For I want you to know exactly how I am placed here. You know the Guild has been in a bad way for a while - well it's likely to be wound up soon and we must either clear out or run a series of shops on our own, renting the places from the Guild, which has the lease. I have been asked to run my little carving shop as my own private concern and for a start I have an organ case to put £150 worth of carving on [this, like the Madona and the Magi, was for the church at Calne]. Well that's a good beginning......I've had what amounted to two offers of work in America - Boston and Cleveland - and there I shall probably go unless there's plenty of good work to keep me here. [Perhaps he really meant, "unless you will come back and marry me".] I must of course see this organ case through......but you'll see in what an unsettled state we are in Campden......The school starts for the winter next Friday and after that I'll have very little time as I have to teach the life class and the elementary drawing - and a carving class at Weston sub Edge. I foresee a busy winter, which is well."

The last letter of that year, written December 15th, says in part:...... "I got run down with an unconscionable amount of work to do, and then Braithwaite had to close up and I had to look out for another place. And then when Mairet[8] and I had taken a small cottage and began to get it in liveable order, suddenly he had to go to London to his father who was dying - and I had to get the house ready in the infinitesimally small amount of spare time classes left me.....but don't think this is a grumble.......I am quite staggered at the thought of your coming home so soon - I wonder if it will really be so.....I have enough work in hand to last me till Easter, and my brother comes South to help me tomorrow. Even yet I can't promise what may happen if no more comes in. I have not given up the idea of Boston!.....This morning CRA and I spent time discussing the problem of how a craftsman can live by his craft and yet away from his clientele - i.e. in the country, not the town. Here is the problem of the Guild, and as you probably know we have practically fizzled out. The Guild of Handicraft Limited goes into liquidation early in the New Year. It is a melancholy thing!....I am.....waiting on here because I have a large order in hand.....I think I can do more than make a wage for myself, Will & Fred. It makes a very great change in one's outlook & gives one far more responsibility than before....."

Eleanor did return from New Zealand, and by August 1908 was back at Saintbury Rectory where the children gave her a rousing welcome. In September, the pair announced their engagement.

Here I will make a short digression and attempt to show the qualities that had been at work in the genesis of Gerald and Eleanor, both of whom played parts in the Campden picture of their time. Eleanor was the thirteenth of the fourteen children of Michael and Alice Bishop, Londoners who eventually moved to Lewes and finally Brighton. They were a lively and enterprising family, of a background very different from that of Alec Miller, or of Ashbee. Their circumstances were not those of wealth, but money evidently was adequate to give a good education to both the boys and the girls. My uncles went to school in Germany for some years, the girls all went to boarding school and my aunt Molly, some ten years older than Eleanor, went on to art school in Paris.

The eldest son became an engineer and went out to South Africa, where he died, leaving a little son. His widow wished the boy to grow up in England, and my grandparents, after fourteen of their own children, took on responsibility for this little grandson, who was ten years younger than Eleanor and only eight years younger than his youngest uncle. I give this sequence because I think it says more about the spirited quality of the Bishop family (and of the parents in particular) than any discursive sentence I could write. In 1910 my father was to execute a portrait of this boy, Jack Bishop. It was his third effort at portraiture, not carved but modelled and coloured. It is a beautiful work, of extraordinary animation.

A collection survives of congratulatory letters on the engagement, sent to Alec in Campden and to Eleanor in Saintbury. Mrs. Mackay wrote to them both, and she evidently visited the Bishops in Brighton in 1908 or '09. My father's eldest sister was shattered at what seemed to her the loss of yet another brother; his brother Jim was delighted. A letter from Phil, one of the Nason children then at school at Christ's Hospital, is so charming that I must transcribe it complete: "My dear Alec I hope you will forgive me for being so long before I answered your letter, I have no time to say much now as I shall be going to tea soon and there are only two weeks and two days before I get home again and then I shall be able to come and see you in your studio, I hope you will come down in the holidays and have some toboganing [*sic*] and come and have supper and that sort of thing. The Examination will soon be on and I hope to come up high in my exams because it all depends on my going into the upper school next term, I am going into the same house Paul is in next term. When are you going to be married to Eleanor, because I should like to be at your wedding and if you write to Eleanor will you please send my best love, I hope you don't mind my saying this. I have nothing more to say so I must end my letter, goodbye for now, ever your loving friend, Phil XXXX P.S. get the studio ready for me please. Also give my love to Fred XXXXX."

Laurence Housman writes characteristically to Eleanor: "I am so very glad to hear that you and Alec have decided to add to the brightness of the world by putting your heads together and becoming a constellation. I suppose to you I ought to say that I congratulate Alec, and to Alec that I congratulate you, but I really congratulate you both about equally. I got the news from Gerald last night: he told me he had been down to Brighton to 'give the young man a good character', and I hear your stern parent insists that it shall not be a long engagement. Oh, if all parents would be stern in the same direction, how much less wearisome courtship there would be in the world....very kind remembrances to the Nasons please. Ever yours brotherly....."

Perhaps my 'stern' grandfather hoped that this youngest daughter's wedding would take place during his wife's lifetime - she was already suffering from cancer - but it was not to be. Alec visited her, and charming letters survive from Alice Bishop to him; but she died in April 1909, Eleanor and her sisters being all at home at the time.

So the wedding of Alec and Eleanor, when it came about in August 1909, was not a Brighton one, nor a Campden one, nor a Saintbury one. I believe that Muriel Nason had reservations about being the celebrant for a Church of England wedding since Alec, grown up in the Baptist tradition, had not been baptised. How this matter was resolved I do not know, but in the event the marriage was performed by Canon Baillie of Rugby (later Dean of Windsor) for whom Alec was executing a large commission that year and who became a lifelong friend and patron. The 'where' resolved itself into the church at St. Nicholas at Wade, a little East Kent village. Here Arthur and Molly Bernhard Smith, Eleanor's brother-in-law and eldest sister, had a little primitive cottage which all the Bishops loved and visited often. Molly proposed that the wedding be held there, feeling - as did Gerald Bishop - responsibly *in loco parentis* to this much younger sister after their mother's death.

The arrangement of sharing a house with 'Pam' Mairet did not last long. In 1908 Alec with his brother Fred moved into 'The Studio' in Calf Lane, now known as 'The Long House', living and working there together and with Will Hart making up 'Messrs. Miller & Hart, Architectural Sculptors & Carvers', as their letterhead read. A note from my father records that 'The Studio', originally a malt barn, was adapted into a dwelling by CRA for George Loosely, a Campden artist but not a member of the Guild. I have some recollection that Fred Griggs also occupied it before the Millers.

Fred Miller was, as I have mentioned, also an ex-apprentice from Mrs. Mackay's studio, and a skilled carver. He worked with Alec on a number of larger commissions such as the work for Calne and for Rugby. In basic decoration I think it would be almost impossible to tell the work of the two brothers apart. Though he never achieved the apparently effortless lyricism which distinguishes Alec's work at its best, Fred kept his love for woodcarving all his life and did several successful portraits.

By early August 1909, letters between the young couple begin to show preoccupation with domestic matters - details of furniture, curtains, luggage and such. Eleanor was familiar with the Studio and its incredible inconvenience as living quarters, but not daunted (and indeed it was their home for 16 years). She writes a humourous note asking Alec to find a certain pair of black shoes known as her 'policeman boots' which she had already sent to the Studio and now has need of in Kent. Then she writes of the arrangements for the wedding and the camping trip they will take afterwards, and also of wedding presents: "If anyone else asks what we want, say some linen sheets and pillow-cases........if it should be a person who would consider linen sheets proper! Glad Canon Baillie was happy at coming. When you write, ask him to verify 9.30 train from Victoria will you? I must book the wagonatte to meet the train [this would have been at Birchington] and take him back. We will walk to our station, Grove Ferry, I think....my big knapsack and the bag and cover - that will do.........I don't think we need take more than the spirit stove and saucepan and cups on this jaunt.....It must seem strange to you, alone in the 'Studium' ....and don't worry dear if things are in a muddle......I won't mind anything - and I am longing to come.......I am so often thinking of mother: it seems so hard she never knew us married......." Later: "Molly and I bearded the sexton in his chuch this morning & booked the church for 12.30 Sat. - told him to open all the windows & door..... old dodderer amused us very much by saying 'You're bringing along your own minister, aren't you?' - sounds as though we'd bring him along in a wheelbarrow!" In the last letter written before Alec set out from Campden for Kent and his wedding, she says "Enclosed is from Mr. Huyshe[9] - which makes me shrivel up. I *told* you I was frightened of Campden *brains*! - & I can't act - but they'll soon find out what an uninteresting and brainless wife you've married.....I'm frightened of these people......" [Huyshe's letter has not survived.]

Then on a totally different topic Eleanor says: "Your thoughtfulness never ends - fancy your thinking of a bathing thing for me, even. How did you know I hadn't one now? Yesterday we had the loveliest bathe and we all - Molly, Hilda, myself, Arthur and Jack bathed with nothinks on.........." [In parentheses, such bathing, 'skinny-dipping' in today's parlance, was still possible and done regularly by Bishops, Bernhard Smiths, Millers and others on that particular beach near the North Foreland throughout the '20s and '30s. It is a matter of laughter to me now to recall those many relations and friends with whom I bathed there as a child - among them well-known artists, a distinguished architect, a famous actor and his actress companion, an American vice-consul and a professor of geography, and all of us of all ages with 'nothinks on' - unless you count the fact that my aunt Molly invariably tied a stocking round her head before plunging into the sea.]

I don't think the Ashbees came to this wedding of their favourite Guildsman; nor, so far as I can ascertain, were any members of Alec's family present. Eleanor's three sisters were there, and at least one brother, Edgar, and nephew Jack. The wedding party elected to walk - bride and all - the short distance down the village street from the Bernhard Smith cottage to the church. The bridegroom and the celebrant, however, arrived by some sort of vehicle.

Poor young Jack had been desolated at the prospect of losing this spirited and companionable aunt - almost his contemporary. It took much reassurance from Alec and Eleanor and a standing invitation that he should come and live with them at the 'Studium' whenever he liked [which in later years he often did] to comfort him - to the point where

"Suppertime at the Studio". My mother attributed this drawing to Fred Griggs,
but I think it must be A.M's work.

he became the life and soul of the wedding celebrations.

The married pair went camping as planned, taking a train from Grove Ferry near St. Nicholas at Wade to Wye, in Kent, on the Pilgrim's Way. Then, brother Fred having moved out of the 'Studium', as they liked to call it, they returned to Campden and took up residence. Initially, as the photographs show, my father used the Studio as a work place as well as living quarters. As his family grew, this proved impracticable and he returned to the Guild building, leasing not the small shop in which he had spent his Guild years but a larger middle-floor shop across from that of the silversmiths.

The drawing on page 26 'Supper time at the Studio' suggests the kind of alfresco living which both Alec and Eleanor enjoyed. In later years my mother attributed this much worn drawing to Fred Griggs, who was indeed a frequent visitor to the Studium and who ate many suppers there; but from the style and the writing of the title I am almost sure it is Alec's work. Whoever drew it, drew with much amusement! Some of the pots and pans I can identify from childhood memories.

Among my father's papers is a copy of an article by F.E.Green, 'The Workshop and the Land', from *The Millgate Monthly*, circa 1910. Its illustrations include a fine wintertime picture of the Studio, showing the numerous fruit trees which were then in the garden.[The caption is inaccurate: The article is especially concerned with the 77 acres acquired and worked by former Guild members, and the value of the relationship between agriculture and handicraft.] Another such article by the same author is entitled 'Village Handicrafts', in *T.P.'s Weekly*. This includes pictures of a number of Alec's works and is of about the same date.

LIFE AND WORK AT THE STUDIO

To be an artist and have the craftsman's trained approach to work, to be hired craftsman and entertain the artist's vision, is to live a peculiar duality without resolution. The quandary is worked out in the stuff of day to day living and earning a living; but society, it seems to me, relentlessly pressures and threatens the balance by which the hapless worker in the field of the arts sustains that duality. Eric Gill, a more vocal, liberated and feisty artist than Alec Miller (and one committed to a creed), has plenty to say about this quandary; Alec's quieter dedication to living it out was, I believe, no less and no less effective than Gill's.

For the ten years from the time he joined the Guild, and indeed in his prior journeyman years also, my father carved whatever he was asked to carve. He met the obligation, whatever he felt about the work - bewilderment at church work given to an unbeliever, longing for "some really pagan work to do" as he rather pathetically mentions in a 1907 letter to Eleanor. (He got plenty of this: a figure of Peter Pan, fauns and other statues for gardens, bird baths and such.) And all the time the search with which every artist is entrusted went on.

Perhaps the demands of this duality were at least ameliorated for Alec when he moved into the field of portraiture (though of course he never did so exclusively). Certainly most of these portraits were commissioned, necessitating satisfying a customer as well as himself, but the best of them - and there are few, if any, failures - make manifest assured, architectonic and lyrical felicity. For Alec Miller perhaps this quality, deriving as it does as much from subject as from workmanship, became more important than what is called 'style'.

My father tells something of what inspired him to portraiture. In writing on his working and student days in Glasgow, he mentions an exhibit at the Art Gallery of medieval wood scupture which included some portraits of Tilman Riemenschneider. Seeing these works was evidently a turning-point for the young man. "These heads filled my mind for days" he wrote "and I returned again and again to see them......though it was 15 years before I ventured on similar portraiture in wood [and got a silver medal from the Worshipful Company of Carpenters for a portrait bust in pearwood] these Riemenschneider heads have always been ....a source of inspiration".

Before the pearwood portrait was carved in 1913, Alec had successfully modelled a few likenesses: a relief of young Phil Nason in 1905, a small - and delightful - head in wax of baby John Ramage, son of Archie Ramage, compositor at the Guild's Essex House Press and a fellow Scot, and a relief medallion of one Jean Hatch. He also in 1910 modelled the remarkable bust of Jack Bishop, mentioned earlier.

In the winter of 1910-1911, thanks to recommendations from Ashbee, Alec and Eleanor left the Studio for Pennsylvania, where Alec fulfilled an important commission - the carving of some 40 stone gargoyles for the cloister at Bryn Mawr College. In the spring of 1911, Eleanor went further West to join her sister Hilda who had been at a sanatorium near Denver, Colorado. Hilda had decided she must leave: the climate and the treatment were not helping her tuberculosis, and she was too ill to travel alone. Eleanor brought her East to New York and thence back across the Atlantic to England and the 'Studium'. For six months the young couple had the care of this sister and sister-in-law who was much loved by both. She was eventually moved to a sanatorium at Bognor, where she died. The first Miller child was born at the Studium in September 1912, a boy whom they named Alastair (for Scotland) William (for his paternal grandfather) Rowsell (for his maternal grandmother whose maiden name it was). Alec modelled a beautiful ten-day-old likeness of this little son.

In the years of the first World War, Alec's scrapbook shows a lot of work for the church and Town Hall at Ulverston, Lancashire, and little else except a carved relief of Peggy Peech, his first commissioned portrait in wood, and a relief of Arthur Geddes, son of Sir Patrick Geddes, done in 1916. I suspect that the Ulverston work kept the wolf from the door in what surely must have been difficult years for the arts.

My father was called up more than once, but rejected for military service on account of a malformed shoulder. His own account of his childhood states that the condition showed itself at about age 14 and was probably the result of too many hours spent at a work bench in the formative years of the bone structure. I remember him commenting once that for maximum skill it was necessary to learn the use of carving tools at a young age, while the wrists are supple, and I am sure this is true. In his case, such learning entailed the unnecessarily long hours which were standard for trade apprentices at that time; he was, quite simply, among the overworked.

My father described to us with amusement a call-up in which he had been included in the later years of the war, when earlier rejects of conscription were being re-evaluated. These Campden men gathered on Honeybourne station, en route to Gloucester and the selection Board. Tom Hook' s sense of comedy took over and he became sergeant, marshalling these rejects with all kinds of infirmities up and down the platform in a parody of drill - Tom himself, as I well remember, being quite lame and having a severely crippled arm and hand. (He kept a little bicycle shop on the Square, and was the kindest of men.)

One big change came about in those years in the circumstances of the Miller family. Cabinet work had dwindled to almost nothing in Glasgow, and Alec's father was persuaded, I believe also with the encouragement of Ashbee, to leave Scotland and move to Campden. This happened in 1915, and my grandparents with their youngest daughter Bessie found a home two doors from the Baptist chapel, on the West side of the square (the house is now an antique shop). William Miller was given shop space at the Guild, and work whenever he was well enough to undertake it. By this time three of his four sons were established in England, Jim being an engineer with the firm of Lucas in Birmingham and Alec and Fred in Campden. Fred Miller was a conscientious objector throughout the war and did land work, subsequently marrying and becoming a teacher of art at a school in Birmingham. His was a Quaker wedding, but Quaker ideas did not prevent my brother and another small boy having to suffer through the ceremony as pageboys in black velvet suits.

The Studio looking North (approximately), 1910

The Studio looking South (approximately), 1910

The Studio has become become living quarters only.
Alec and Eleanor with Alastair, 1915

Drawing by Alec Miller of his son, Douglas,
who was born in 1916 and died in 1918

My grandfather died in 1918, and is buried in Campden churchyard. Alec carved the very simple tombstone, and added to it his mother's name after her death in 1931. It is curious that they are buried under the wing of the Church of England, since they were lifelong dissenting chapel-goers and Campden Baptist chapel had a graveyard at that time, but so it was, and I remember my mother telling me that the choice was a very definite one on the part of Grannie.

One would be hard put to it today even to imagine the inconveniences of life at the Studio - let alone to deal with them on a daily basis. The main room was something like 60 feet long and extremely high, with two huge sky-lights to the North; superb light for an artist, but impossible to heat. At each end a room had been partitioned off, the one to the West, extremely dark, being a bedroom and that to the East a sitting-room with some semblance of conventionality. Steps from this room led down into the garden. For another entrance to the big studio room, one plunged into the cellar by a door on the South side and thence up some dark stairs with a curtain hung across at the top - an attempt to exclude at least some of the draughts which played around the barn-like space.

By the time I myself came to consciousness in the early 1920s, there was some plumbing at the Studio. The 'kitchen' at the East end, alongside the sitting-room, had a sink with a cold tap, and a bathroom had been partitioned off in the Southwest corner of the main studio. My recollection is that this had a basin with a tap and a bath into which cold water could be brought up by a pump installed at one end. I hardly think these cold water improvements did much to mitigate the discomforts with which my mother and her occasional helper or nurse had to deal daily. She had three babies at the Studio, and I was the last to be born in that dark bedroom, being delivered by a Doctor Alexander who rode over from Broadway on horseback for the occasion. He was almost too late, and my mother laughed at him.

That was in August 1917. Before that, in 1915, my parents's second child, a little boy whom they called Douglas, had been born, with a cleft palate and a very much enlarged heart. He was expected to die within a week, then within a month, then within a year. However, he lived until May 1918, being in the last year under the care of nurses in the household of Dr. Maude Royden in London. Dr. Royden was a devout Anglican who, after doing settlement work in Liverpool and also lecturing on Oxford University Extension Courses, became assistant preacher at the City Temple. With Percy Dearmer she founded the Fellowship Services which eventually found a home at the Guildhouse, Eccleston Square. She was a frequent visitor to Campden with Ashbees and Millers, and she had participated in at least one of the Guild plays. I have a very vivid memory of her, dating from about 1926 or so - a splendid woman with a deep voice, sitting in the firelight and holding forth to my parents on what seemed to her to be the iniquities of spiritualism. She made an enormous impression on one young girl, and I think I had some intimation of human greatness. But I knew nothing then of what she had done for my parents and their little son whose passage was so brief.

"THROUGH THE EYES OF A CHILD"

How can I evoke the quietness and simplicity of our lives in Campden during my childhood? My particular world was triangulated by the Studio, my father's shop at the Guild and my grandmother's house on the Square. From a very early age I moved freely about the village alone, but I never objected to those times when I was supposed to stay in the Studio garden. For one thing, there were chickens in a run in one corner, and in another was that place of mysterious friendliness - the outhouse, buried in ivy, with a scrubbed wood seat, a tiny window and a block of pink disinfectant hung in a wire cage on the wall. Also, there were the cellars. In the first were kept gardening tools and such and the scratch feed for the chickens. It was an endless joy to me to run this through my hands, feeling and examining the variety of grains and picking out the wheat which was just not too hard for my small teeth. In the second cellar space was coal and a coal hammer, and to break the big lumps into smaller lumps was my special pleasure. I am grateful to my mother that she allowed this occupation at which I must often have acquired very dirty clothes - to say nothing of mashed fingers and thumbs, for the hammer was a heavy one.

I remember well our bedroom which had one high, yew-tree-filled window and in which we all slept, my parents in a bed of my grandfather's making and my brother and myself on slatted cots - perhaps he had made these too. In that room I acquired literacy. Alastair and I had been through a bout of polio together and bookseller Basil Blackwell, a good friend of my father's, knowing we were housebound sent us a splendid parcel of books, including the three volumes of fairy stories by Laurence Housman. The joy we had in these stories is with me still. I read them and re-read them until, with my father's help, I had mastered all the long words and difficult names (I hardly think those stories were written with child readers in mind). Before this encounter, I could read; after, I could navigate, however

35

Eleanor with Jane in the Studio
garden, c. 1920

Alastair with Mary and Felicity Ashbee,
c. 1917

Children at a party given by Mr & Mrs Robert Cust, Campden c.1925. Back:
Alastair Miller, Theodore Budgen, 3 unknown, Margaret Hart. Middle: Michael
Blair Fish, unknown, Jane Miller, Charmian Orpen, Joan Brooks, Desmond
Pyment, Virginia Orpen, Ann Blair Fish. Seated: Boy in sailor suit was son of
Lloyds Bank Manager. The other three unknown. The Budgens, Blair Fishes and
Orpens all lived in Broad Campden

inexpertly, on the limitless sea of books and newspapers, and I developed some sort of poetic sense - largely thanks to my brother, in whom this faculty was strong.

To reach the Studio from the High Street, one opened the door of the 'Swan' passage, went past the entrance to a little oil and plumbing shop, and then plunged through darkness to emerge close to the Studio gate in Calf Lane, which was paved - if one could call it paving - with cinders only, and frequently very muddy. Other ways, in addition of course to the turning at the top of Church Street, were through the 'Live and Let Live' passage or, as today, through the yard of the Lygon Arms or Noel Arms Hotel. But it was the 'Swan' passage that we used most.

In my early years, the mill on the lane off Calf Lane was still working. The big water-wheel was to me a terror and a fascination; when I heard it turning I always wanted to go and watch it and yet was uncertain about going alone. I felt safer with my mother, and she was on good terms with miller Dudley Haydon. True to the riddle, he did wear a white cap, and was floury from head to foot. The noise inside the mill was thunderous and it was awesome to watch the great shaft and the millstone turning - but it was the huge and slimy water-wheel outside which really gave me a feeling of fear.

On the whole, though, there was little in Campden that engendered fear, even in a small child. I was a little intimidated by meeting Charlie Seitz, especially if I encountered him alone when he was homeward bound with some enormous load of wood on his back, making him look about ten feet tall - but my parents had told me always to greet him, which I did, and he always responded. As I recall he was connected with the Izod family. He had been born in India, returned to Campden and fell on bad times and illness and was pretty much disowned. A tall, striking figure, dressed literally in rags, he lived and died as an indigent in Broad Campden (Graham Greene gives a good picture of him in *A Sort of Life*). He tramped for miles in search of fuel, and indeed many in Campden did so; in autumn one might meet families returning from Weston Woods with faggots piled high on an old pram and children following, each with a load on arm or back.

I was familiar with other Campden 'characters', among them

'Teapot'[10] and the famous Bob Dickinson[11] and his wife who lived in Cider Mill Lane, and of course Mr. George Haysum, driver of the bus which made daily trips to the station. I have one memory of going with him in his horse bus, which I should think by that time in the 20s must have been already a museum piece - but mostly I remember the rackety motor bus and how my father always worried that Haysum would be late for the train and yet he never was, though he sometimes cut things very fine. In later years, when I was going regularly by train to Oxford for art classes, I rode my bicycle to the station, left it for the day and saved my sixpence.

The periodic market day in the Square was always an excitement, and a meet of the Hunt doubly so. Scuttlebrook Wake[12] of course dominated everyone's thinking for weeks before it was held - and for days afterward. An occasional small circus or barnstorming group caused some excitement. I remember being taken by my father to see *Maria Marten, or the Murder in the Red Barn* acted by a travelling troupe in a tent in Badger's field. The footlights were a row of lamps and our seats were benches set of course right on the ground so that our feet got very cold. I cannot have been more than six and I understood little if any of the plot, but the thrill of being out at night made it a memorable event.

In those years the ruins of Campden House[13] were accessible and the pavilions open and used for farm storage, and the whole area made a splendid playground. I especially liked to go down to Lady Juliana's gateway and then explore along the stream.

At the Guild I had friends: Mr. Pyment[14] and his sons, Harold and Arthur, silversmiths George Hart and Harry Warmington and later Jack Davis, and also Charlie Downer and Bill Thornton in the blacksmith's shop. These men were all patient with a wandering child. Understandably enough, it was among the woodworkers that I felt especially at home, and from them I received a sort a freedom of the city - from the lumber shed at the back of the Guild grounds to the cabinetmaker's shop on the top floor. I liked to venture into the lumber shed, where seasoning wood of all kinds and dimensions was stored vertically. I made my way in and out of the clumps as one might wander in a forest - and to a small child the place was like a forest,

Grannie Miller at the Studio with Jim, Alec, Eleanor,
Maggie (Jim's wife) Bessie with Alastair c. 1917

Summer School teachers: Will Hart,
George Hart, Alec Miller,
William Mark

Alec MIller,
Justice of the Peace, 1924

fragrant and tall. No-one minded if I turned the handle of the big grindstone in the yard, which could be operated by treadle also. The stone revolved through most satisfactorily dirty water.

My father's shop was quite large and had windows on two sides, with lengths of bench space under them and all the equipment of his sculptor's trade to hand. In one corner was a stone sink with a cold tap, and in the centre a low coke-burning stove which in cold weather could be fired up to a most comforting heat and on which my father put a ruinous old kettle to make himself an afternoon cup of tea, having brought with him from home a little botttle of milk for this, and a bun or such to accompany it - what the Scots called a 'piece'. Invariably on the job he wore a faded blue smock, copied from that of the French *ouvrier*, almost down to his knees and with long sleeves. In later years he sometimes would settle for a blue chinese coat. His was a friendly spirit, patient with visitors and droppers-in whether neighbours or people from afar, young or old, knowledgeable or not. One form of interruption I think he did grudge somewhat: he had been made a Justice of the Peace in 1924 and was often unmindful of Court day - and then in the midst of work would suddenly remember, say "Drat it!" and have to pull off his smock and comb his hair and go off to 'sit on the Bench'. More than once he amused my mother by setting out to fulfil this obligation while wearing corduroy shorts - a form of dress he liked and about which he was quite unselfconscious. If the Chairman disapproved, I think nothing was ever said.

There were other ways in which my father and his family did not quite conform. There was, for instance, the matter of my education. Though my brother, after a start in Ethel Hands' little class along with the Ashbee girls, went off to a boarding preparatory school and then to Bembridge School on the Isle of Wight, I somehow was never sent to school anywhere, and Sup. Jones or some other representative of the law called, I think twice a year, to verify that I was receiving an education, my father signing an affidavit to that effect. I can't remember a time when I couldn't read, and I did get more or less educated, starting also with Ethel Hands as teacher and eventually achieving a school leaving certificate, but was never enrolled in any school. I regret that through this decision I knew so few of my Campden contemporaries.

Then there was the constant problem of riding a bicycle without the required light. As I mentioned earlier, my father used a bicycle to go back and forth between home and shop, and often stayed unexpectedly late at work and found himself without a lamp and so rode home with none. I recall his coming in late one winter night, much amused by the village constable who had tactfully stooped to tie a shoelace while the J.P. rode illegally by. In those days a bicycle lamp meant just that - not a battery-powered torch but a lamp, so that one had to remember to keep it filled, trim the wick and always carry matches.

Very early I learned, as had my brother before me, the names and uses of my father's many tools and pieces of equipment - calipers, clamps, different kinds of vise, mallets and hammers, spokeshaves, saws and the huge assortment of chisels, gouges and v tools, each in a different type of wood handle. There was a revolving modeling stand, a drawing table, drawing boards, T squares and try squares. There were paints and brushes, turpentine and methylated spirits and shellac. I was eager to watch any process at any time! I learned the basic techniques of woodcarving, and of stone carving too, and as I grew older was entrusted with some easy, repetitive work - a length of decorated frame for a tablet or something like that. I washed brushes and swept the benches and floor, no doubt quite inefficiently, and turned the handle of the carborundum wheel while my father expertly held his chisel to it, producing in the process splendid showers of sparks. I have already mentioned what a master he was at sharpening any tool. Only occasionally when a blade had been used or misused for unduly rough work was it necessary to apply it to the wheel. In general, the oilstone was sufficient, followed by a brisk stropping on a leather razor strop. The result was a blade which would respond to almost any demand. I remember one summer evening when my mother complained of a troublesome corn and my father carved it out painlessly, using a small gouge and holding her foot firmly between his knees.

Upstairs again, at the top of the Guild building, was the cabinetmaking shop of Bill Wall and Arthur Bunten, both of whom had been Guild members and both of whom I loved. Here was the same kind of arrangement as on the floor below, only with more benches, some free-standing as well as under the windows, a larger and more

41

decrepit stove, an even more disgraceful sink in one corner and beside it a gas-ring on which an outrageously-smelling glue pot simmered all day long. Around 1929 or so I had, with another girl, Elizabeth Devas from Broad Campden, the privilege of carpentry lessons with Bill Wall. I believe my mother was the prime mover in this, knowing that Bill and Arthur had all too little work coming in during that rather lean time and so might have hours to spare and be glad of a little extra money. Bill was patient, and we did learn a lot from him, but I know the whole business tried his soul and I recall well a suffering and yet friendly sigh from him accompanied by the words "What am I doing - teaching little girls to make furniture!" It was a long-drawn-out and very expressive plaint, with a semblance of outrage on top and goodwill underneath.

I think above all I learned that workmanship in the arts and crafts involved the skilled whole person; that without that total physical and mental rapport, authentic work would not emerge. I saw Bill Wall, in the white apron he always wore over his work clothes, using a brace and bit over a low bench, grasping the top of the brace with his left hand and leaning his venerable forehead on that hand as he turned the brace with his right, and every bit of body and soul intent on drilling to prefection. I saw my father, given to the delicate task of laying gold leaf, rub two small brushes through his hair to create static electricity in them and render them capable of picking up the sheet of gold by the corners without its folding. Then, the sheet was almost breathed into place on a surface already made tacky with shellac. The concentration with which such comparatively small processes were carried out was no less than that exercised in the use of a tackle and hoist, or of a two-man saw - which I also remember watching when work was done in the shed in the yard behind the Guild. When such skills are at work, you know you are in the presence of *homo faber*, and that he is to be deeply respected.

At my grandmother's house other things were to be observed and learned. Grannie's life, organised around the services and activities of the neighbouring Baptist chapel, was as different from the bohemianism of the Studio as one could possibly imagine. With my aunt Bessie, she kept house with a decorum that was fascinating to me as a small child - though I realise now that my father was glad to be free of it. He faithfully stopped by almost every day to see his mother, and

Grannie Miller with grand daughter Jane, c. 1922

my mother also was very conscientious about visiting and in seeing that Alastair and I frequently did likewise. I loved to go to tea there, and my very earliest memory is of walking along the upper side of the Square bound for Grannie's house, carrying a little blue-enamelled can of milk for my tea. My mother always sent me with this, knowing well that there were no extra pennies for extra milk in that house. I know now that my grandmother had only her 'Lloyd George' pension of 10/- a week; her sons between them supplied whatever else was needed for this very frugal, careful mother-and-daughter household. And it *was* careful! - though it never felt mean. I don't know what the rent was. Their landlord was Mr. Ebborn who lived next door, and they had the use of a plot of ground up towards Back Ends which contained wonderful gooseberry and raspberry bushes.

Every piece of coal was thought about before being placed on the fire, and I have never forgotten Grannie teaching me to make spills of folded newspaper. One of these, lit at the hearth, was used to light the gas lamps or stove, so that the striking of a match was necessary perhaps only once a day. Every stratagem of thrift was employed in that little house. I do not mean to imply that thrift was not practised in our house also, for indeed it was, and frugality prevailed in a way almost incomprehensible today - but the style was different, and there was something about the proportional orderliness at Grannie's that made a great appeal to me. Alastair and I thought the tea-time ritual very wonderful, with the cloth laid meticulously cornerwise on the table, a doily beneath the plate of scones and a grace whispered over the teacups. Grannie's potato scones, with her gooseberry jam, were a feast.

The front room, facing nearly on the Square, had a fireplace with a copper hearth fender on which was embossed 'The fire is the flower of the winter's day'. I thought this beautiful - and so it was, especially after my aunt Bessie had polished it. There was a piano, never played, a glass-fronted bookcase, a small armchair and Grannie's larger one, and beside it her work table with her rug-making equipment on it. The window had a built-in seat and here in winter I would go after tea because, just as in Stevenson's poem, there was a street lamp just outside and sure enough in my earliest years here would come the lamplighter with his ladder to light the gas, then passing on to the next lamp outside the Town Hall. I have forgotten his name. To me this was 'city life' for we had no gas at the Studio and no street lights in Calf Lane.

There was a back room used for meals, a further back kitchen and a freezing further back scullery with a stone sink and a copper and a toilet in an ultimate dark cupboard. Upstairs were two bedrooms, Grannie slept in the front one, and all the furniture in it had been made by my grandfather. The wardrobe had a carved panel done, I think, by my uncle Fred, depicting a woman holding a hand mirror and having the inscription 'Self love is not so vile a sin as self neglect'. I must have been a child receptive to aphorisms, for I recall these so clearly - and another more usual one done in water-colour and hanging in the narrow hallway: 'Let him that hath two loaves sell one and buy anemones, for bread is the food of the body but flowers are the food of the soul.' I doubt if Grannie ever had that second loaf; but I was often sent by my mother to pick early primroses or the first bluebells and to take them to Grannie's house. For primroses and anemones we went to Weston Woods and for bluebells to the Linches where they grew in a profusion nothing less than divine. Later in the year we got cowslips from a field near Gun's cottages on the way to Willersey. In autumn, for Grannie's November birthday, we looked for spindleberry near the site of the Kiftsgate stone and for crab apples from an old tree on Conduit Hill.

Grannie had a fund of stories based on her difficulties with English language and Scots usage when she first came to England. She asked Walter Keen, the milkman who drove the milk cart for Haines' Westington farm, to bring her six eggs the next day. "Ye'll mind, now, Walter?" she had called to him (meaning, "You'll remember?"). "Oh no, ma'am, I won't mind at all" responded Walter as he drove off - and Grannie retreated indoors in laughter.

Starting, I think, in 1919, when the War was over, their grief at the loss of their little boy fading and their new baby thriving, Alec and Eleanor instituted what became a nearly annual festivity: a fancy-dress party, for which they hired the Town Hall. (I was eight or nine before I attended one of these). Grannie had been greatly disapproving of this very frivolous prospect, but was eventually persuaded to put aside her prejudices and attend the first party. My mother had the Hall floor thoroughly scrubbed beforehand, and then polished, and the two fireplaces which provided the only heat had to be generously fuelled and blazing. To cap these festive proceedings, my parents served a claret cup - heaven alone knows it would have been mild enough, but it was alcoholic and I'm sure Grannie had a hard time being in the same room with it. Beside one of the fireplaces Grannie was installed, to watch or at least endure the dancing. As the evening wore on, her feelings mellowed, partly because she very much liked Mrs. Nason who played the piano for the affair, and at the end she told my mother, in her strongly Scots speeech: "I've made a great mistake. I always thought there was sin in dancing, and now I see there is not. Bessie must learn". My mother always had a real affection for her mother-in-law, and perhaps never more than at that moment. She recounted the story more than once, and always with pleasure. Grannie came, with a soft white shawl over her black dress, to every dance that I can remember, often sitting with Miss Josephine Griffiths, who also never missed attending.

I have wandered afield in childhood impressions, in the hope that some of them may show something of the Campden milieu in which Alec Miller, with his family, lived and worked. There was another locale which was important to him, and before resuming a more formal perspective I think I should try to touch on it. In St. Nicholas at Wade, where they had been married, my parents acquired a quarter acre about 1920 or 21, and put a surplus army hut on it. We were to spend many summer weeks there, over the years, close to the Bernhard Smiths in their cottage which adjoined a farmyard. Sometimes my father could join us only briefly, but there were some summers when he brought work with him and stayed perhaps six weeks. He sought the use of a bench and vise for occasional hours in the village carpenter's shop where he was always much welcomed. After work, or sometimes before, depending on the state of the tide, we would set off across the marshes to the beach, I riding on the bar or the carrier of my father's bicycle. We took food and water for the day and one of the pleasures was to make a driftwood fire and boil a kettle on it for after-bathing tea. And the bathing! - but I have already described that.

The St. Nicholas carpenter's shop had been a wheelwright's, and was equipped to repair if not to build the huge Kentish farm wagons which were still in use there in the '20s. Across the road was the blacksmith's shop where the great carthorses stood patiently, each waiting to receive a "bright and battering sandal". The ancient red brick walls of the village, the grey flint church and the tarred wood farm buildings were a remarkable contrast to Campden. I was at home in both villages, and remember gratefully the splendid Kentish cornfields edged with brilliant poppies growing close to our 'hutment', the ring of the blacksmith's hammer which began in the very early morning, and visiting a cottage which belonged to a shepherd - thatched, with a quarried floor and a well surrounded by hollyhocks in the garden. My delight was to watch the bucket go down and to see it come up brimming from mysterious depths that I did not understand.

There was one year when my father was carving two fairly small standing figures for a memorial and, not needing a bench, simply worked at home with the wood, fastened to a device he called a 'bridge', on his knees. That was the summer C.R.Ashbee came to stay for a couple of weeks. I resented the way he monopolised my father, but he made peace with me by giving me a copy of Walter Crane's *Flora's Feast* - which I still have.

Of course, below the 'simple life' in both villages lay all the inescapable and powerful workings of the economy, the social forces and the individual characters. I think my father was well-liked by most and loved by many, and his position, if that is the word, as artist kept him free from any definable social stratum or any particular clique, wherever he went. In the quietness - and I cannot stress that quality too much - of Campden life, my father put in tremendously long hours of devoted craftsmanship, always six and sometimes seven days a week and with a drive and willingness that surely must have amazed some of his customers and patrons. He also became a much sought-after lecturer, about which aspect of his vocation I will tell later.

In the 1920s much of Alec Miller's commissioned work consisted of the carving of war memorials, often of stone, sometimes simply wood tablets to be installed in churches. Invariably - how could it be otherwise - this was sad work for my father; though he put all the heart into it that he could. He carved the cross for Saintbury in 1920, and the Campden war memorial is listed in his far from complete record book as "Designed by F.L.Griggs, The whole of the carving was the work

The "Franz Hals Baby", 1918. Exhibited at the XXI Gallery, 1920

"Joy of Life".
Exhibited at the XXI Gallery, 1920

Portrait of Jack Bishop
(a "Bluecoat Boy") 1910
This is not carved but modelled in clay

and gift of Alec Miller, done in Campden stone, 1921-22". Other memorials of his carving in the region are at Shipston-on-Stour, Aston, Broadway, Willersey, Bourton-on-the-Water, Snowshill, Cleeve, Chedworth, Cirencester, Blockley, Bicester and Oxford. In St. James' Church, Campden, is a carved figure on a priedieu, and in St. Catharine's Church is a large crucifix on the rood screen, again designed by F.L.Griggs. I believe both of these date from the 1920's.

My mother's eldest sister, Mrs. Molly Bernhard Smith, gave Alec Miller his first one-man show at her XXI Gallery on Durham House Street, Adelphi, in April 1920. The catalogue lists twenty-six exhibits, including 'Bluecoat Boy', which is the portrait of Jack Bishop, 'Portrait bust of a boy' in limewood, which is my brother Alastair at age 7, 'St. Chad' cast in bronze, and 'Puck' in stone. This last was a garden figure and was exhibited at the Royal Academy the following year, and sold. Its present whereabouts are not known to me, but he carved a second version some years later which has recently found a home in Evesham. It has also been discovered lately that Mr. Desmond Pyment has one in his garden in Campden.

My aunt's gallery was well-known, and though she specialised in prints and etchings (and consistently showed work by F.L.Griggs) press coverage of this modest sculpture exhibition was good. There were notices with illustrations in the Morning Post, the Daily Mirror, the Daily Sketch, the Evening Standard, the Builder and other publications, not identified. One reviewer commented: "Alec Miller's woodcarving is astonishingly bold and effective.....Mr. Miller does not indeed confine himself to sculpture in wood, for we find among his material bronze, stone, alabaster, wax and plaster; the work in different woods is.......predominant and interesting.......his brilliant advancing figure of 'The Joy of Life' is really a *tour de force* in this material for we must remember that a single false movement of the tool would have spoilt the piece.........Next to this, I should place the stone figure of 'Puck'......." Another wrote: "The attractive possibilities of carving in various woods are indicated by the artist, who is supremely successful in a series of portraits and religious subjects.....Particularly alluring is a statuette in limewood of a charming and distinctly Franz Hals baby". Such is my claim to fame, for I was that baby!

THE WORKMAN AND HIS WORK

Alec had work in the Royal Academy exhibition in 1922 - and in almost every year throughout the '20s - and a one-man exhibition in Glasgow. That year also saw the completion of the largest single piece of wood sculpture he ever undertook. This was a more-than-life-size statue of Saint Michael for Coventry Cathedral, and was also a war memorial. The design included a large commemorative panel below a plinth set high on a wall on which the statue was installed. I do not know where he obtained the enormous piece of teak wood out of which he carved this figure. It was two feet square by nine feet in length, and of excellent quality. The first two days of work on it were done with a two-man saw, and for weeks he was using only his very largest chisels and gouges.

The right arm of the heroic armoured figure is upraised and holding a sword, and since the teak was not quite long enough for this, the upper portion of the arm was carved separately and fitted and pegged into the lower part. The sword also was made separately and fitted to the hand and the upraised wings, again carved from other pieces of wood, were when finished screwed to the back, making the total height of the figure nearly eleven feet, with the tip of the sword even higher.

To the best of my recollection, the whole of the main figure was carved and painted in the shed in the Guild back yard. It took many weeks, and was a commission which generated much interest in Campden. People dropped by to watch the appearance, day by day, of a figure on such an unusually large scale, and my brother and I were not the only children to be found, perhaps all too often, hanging around the yard. How it was taken to Coventry, and by whom, I do not remember, but I would suppose that Pyment's undertook what certainly must have been a transportational challenge.

Alec Miller with statue of St. Michael, carved for Coventry Cathedral, 1922

The whole work was completely destroyed in the 1940 air raid on Coventry in World War II, and with it went seven screens, an altar cross in the Children's Chapel and a carved Bishop's throne, all of my father's workmanship. "Seven years of my work were included in that destruction", he was to say.

The Cathedral authorities wrote to him immediately and asked him to undertake replacement after the war. He agreed, but when eventually rebuilding was begun he was nearly seventy and living on the other side of the world, and he felt it was not feasible to take on the task of a second St. Michael. He did however carve a replica of the cross for the Children's Chapel, for which he still had the working drawings. This he did in Santa Barbara, California, and it was included in an exhibition there before being shipped to Coventry.

In the course of the 1920's, Alec Miller had two apprentice-assistants, Edgar Keene and Jack Brookes. Whether Edgar helped him on the St. Michael I cannot remember, but I know he was around the shop at that time and in late 1923 tried to emigrate to the United States only to be turned back at Ellis Island as the quota was full. He returned to Campden and my father was happy to have him back as a lot of work had come in during his absence, and Alec himself was also contemplating, not emigration, but at least a trip to the States. Eventually, Edgar did succeed in his plan to move to America, making a living by carving and teaching carving. In later years Edgar's parents lived in the Almshouses, which is all I can recollect of his family.

The other assistant, Jack Brookes, went on to a distinguished career as teacher of art and eventually was principal of the Oxford City School of Art, later the College of Technology, Art and Commerce. [It is now the Oxford Brookes University, formed in 1991, and named after him. Ed.] Jack was not, like Edgar, a Campden native but spent a number of years there, and my father carved a beautiful little relief portrait of his daughter Joan.

During the winter of 1923-4, my father carved a piece in basswood which he named 'Family Group'. It is something of a tour-de-force, an ingeniously composed grouping some 21 inches high, comprising my mother seated in an armchair, myself on her lap and my brother

A. M. studies a young subject for portrait

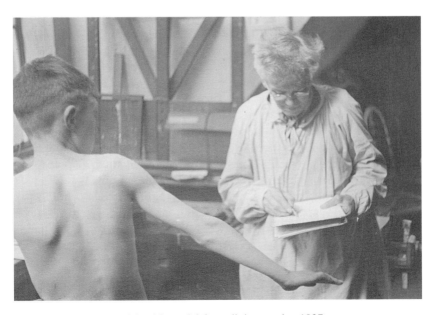

A. M. with model for a diving trophy, 1937

beside her. The latter wears the kilt, an effective element in the design. It fell to my mother to take this work to London for submission to the Royal Academy, since my father left in March on a three-month trip to the United States. The Academy accepted the piece, and it received a good deal of attention in the 1924 Exhibition.

Alec had been encouraged to try his luck in the States by Wendell Herbruck, an American who had visited Campden while a student at Oxford and had become deeply interested in Alec Miller's work and ideas. Wendell had returned to his home in Canton, Ohio, and was in a thriving law practice by 1924. He promised portrait commissions and lecture assignments. My parents were at the time, after 15 years in the 'Studium', contemplating the possibility of having a house built, and the prospect of a profitable trip to the United States seemed very appealing. This one was to be the first of many, for as portraitist and lecturer my father found himself much in demand, and U.S. fees were more generous than he could command in England at that time.

The Canton Sunday paper of April 1924 printed an enthusiastic piece of journalism headlined "FAMOUS BRITISH SCULPTOR HERE TRANSFORMS BLOCK OF WOOD INTO HEAD OF CHILD WHILE AT PLAY: works in playroom at home of Wendell Herbruck". The article below the headline is a comedic mixture of sensitivity and journalese. "It was fascinating to watch the man at work as he sat in the little girl's playroom with the afternoon sun streaming in on his shoulders and on the child's face that was appearing almost miraculously in the wood block on his knees.....Before him on a table that has served more than once for a little girl's tea party lay the tools which wrought in the wood like magic. The sculptor.....worked rather from an indelible impression of the child in his memory than actually from the child as she played near him....He never asks his models to sit immovable in a particular pose.....He works rapidly: two hours after the block of poplar had been attacked by the little tools, an indisputable likeness of small Caroline was there. Not for longer than two or three hours does he pursue his subject without a rest period. 'If one works too long, presently one sees nothing at all. It is better to stop and rest a bit and refresh oneself', he said".

I quote from the more accurate parts of this article. And I quote it

Caroline, daughter of Wendell
Herbruck, Canton, Ohio.
Carved in yellow poplar. 7" high. 1924
The portrait the Cleveland reporter
wrote about

Peter Clayton, Yellow poplar, 1925

Alice Byrd. Limewood, 1927

Peter Bull, Yellow poplar, 1927

because, uninformed and fulsome though it may be and written very far from Campden, it is a sincere and partly successful try at describing the requirements of portrait sculpture. The writer states that the sculptor 'worked rather from an indelible impression of the child in his memory than actually from the child'; it would be more accurate to say that he worked from a whole set of multi-faceted impressions, which were to be held in the mind simultaneously. But this journalist is right in making clear that for my father the essential, key condition for portraiture was the companionable presence of the child, making possible intense observation but asking for no posing. He always did some very careful measuring with calipers - a process intriguing to children - and translated his measurements to a drawn scale, but he did not make drawings of the child. He spent time quite unobtrusively studying characteristics - how the head was typically held, how the ears related to the face, how the eyebrows worked, the texture of the hair - and then, as the Canton writer said, hold these in mind while his tools "attacked" the wood. It is right to say that the likeness often appeared in an incredibly short time, such as two hours, but my father liked to have at least a week in company with his subject. Truly, his power of accurate observation was phenomenal, especially when one remembers how particularly elusive, evanescent and mutable are the forms of childhood, and his skill in translating such observation into sculpture quite extraordinary.

The trip to the States lasted until June. It included a one-man show at the Fitzroy Carrington Galleries and another at the Cleveland Museum of Art, and a number of lectures and portrait commissions besides that of Caroline Herbruck. When he returned to Campden, the site was ready for the building of the new house, up on the 'bank' where what was then called Watery Lane, now Park Road, becomes Dyers Lane. Some time before the end of 1924, the move from the Studio was accomplished. I believe it was in that same year that the portrait of Peter Clayton, whose family lived in Broad Campden, was carved - one of the most splendidly characterful portraits that my father did. (In the 1950s he was to write that he had done "at least 200", and I suspect that is a conservative estimate. Some future art historian may enjoy an inter-continental hunt from which to base a comprehensive record of Alec Miller's work).

"Atalanta". Carved in limewood 1933.
Exhibited at the Royal Academy Now in Cleveland, Ohio Museum of Art.

Arthur Brampton of Broad Campden,
Limewood, 1928

R. Ellis Roberts, c 1947-48

I am not clear as to how many times Alec crossed the Atlantic during the '20s, but there were at least three trips before 1929, which was the year when my mother finally said "This time we're all going", - and so we did, landing in New York on the very day of the stockmarket crash.

With each trip my father of course made more contacts and more friends, some of whom became lifelong and dear to him, such as Christopher Morley, Dr. Ludlow Bull of New York's Metropolitan Museum and Theodore Sizer and his family of Cleveland and later of Yale University. Though there was always a trickle of work in England there was something more like a spate in the United States even in the depression years and, more important, there was I think more stimulus for my father and more interest in his ideas and his particular *genre*.

Some letters of my grandmother's written to us in America during that winter of 1929-30 have survived. She writes from Campden of much severe weather: "You were fortunate going when you did as the storms began the day after your sailing and have continued more or less ever since......The cold is severe but we have kept good fires when we could.....Your logs help and of course some of the coal is lovely and we are thankful to have it and well we may be when so many are without......I am so glad you all keep well and ....also learn that Alec has so much work ahead of him......May you be spared to come back again and if it be the Lord's will to let us meet once more we shall give Him our sincere thanks......"

A little note to my brother, then 17, reads: "My dear Alistair it was cheerful news that you gave me of your job in a bookshop.....I hope you have been a persuasive salesman and managed to sell well. I would just love to see you getting home with your first pay of £3 it is a big one, very different from your father's and uncles'.....Have you had any skating or sledging yet we have had heavy ground frost & fog but no snow to speak of........."

Nobody was more glad than Grannie to see us all back in Campden in the spring of 1930. She died the next year, looked after to the end by her faithful daughter Bessie. My father was in bed with severe flu at the time of her death, but got up to attend the funeral and my brother and I went with him. After the service in the Baptist chapel, the elm coffin was put on a handcart and quietly taken through the town to the churchyard. We did not follow it, for my father was feverish and shivering, and it was a bitterly cold day.

In a recent book on work *per se* - a subject too seldom addressed - the following definition is given: 'Human work is the preservation and enhancement of shared skills.'[15] This definition makes clear what is inhuman work, and also makes room for the work of the artist and intellectual without setting him or her apart from the generality of labour. The positive inclusiveness of the definition would I think have satisfied my father, for the 'preservation and enhancement of shared skills', mostly in a historical context, was often the subject of the lectures which he gave both in England and America. They contain much of his thought on art, and the reiterated message contained in them is simple: cultural history is in the hands of the worker.

Even the title of Alec Miller's lectures convey the message - Art as a spiritual force, A sculptor's view of history, Franciscan ideals in relation to art, History as workmen made it, The Renaissance: its gains and losses. On this last topic he maintains that the Renaissance tended to substitution of scholarship for workman's traditions, to the impoverishment of some aspects of culture. And on the subject of Architecture, 'The Mistress Art', he has challenging things to say about its relationship to sculpture and the changes that occurred when architecture became a 'profession' rather than a skill.

A lecture on 'The Craftsman - his Education and his place in Industry' given at an educational conference in Cambridge in 1919, opens characteristically - "You may justly be suspicious when a workman forsakes his overall for the mantle of a preacher. I can only plead that I don't do it often, and that I welcome this opportunity to present to an audience such as this the workman's point of view". In this lecture Alec makes a case, rooted in history, for education based on working, unifying experience: ".......The large shop with its subdivision of labour, the art school with its theories and compartments - these must be broken down because they perpetuate the false distinction between the designer and the workman, the studio and the workshop..... Let them scrap the elaborate designs for ill-understood processes......and let the students make the chairs and tables and paint pots and aprons, and instead of a long series of drawings of 'The Cup through the Ages' let them make a cup and saucer of real clay - and the link with the past will be through the hand as well as the head, and they will share with God the joy of creation".

Plainly, it was from a strong working identity that such statements were made, by one who, as it were, left his bench briefly to deliver the message, only to turn thankfully back to the task at hand. The quality of immediacy was effective, as the following quotations show.
Professor (later Sir) Patrick Geddes writes of Alec Miller as speaker: ".......his expressions are not simply those of good taste and experienced connoisseurship, but spring direct from his own life-work as craftsman.......Too commonly as yet the teacher, however scholarly and critical, cannot create - while the creative artist is usually obliged to leave his work to speak for itself. But here is one of the few living men who combine both aptitudes, of thought and deed, in high degree".
Maude Royden says: "Mr. Alec Miller's lectures on art are quite unlike any others I have ever heard: perhaps because it is extremely rare for the artist and the speaker to be combined in one person.....Mr. Miller.....speaks of what he knows at first and not second hand.....this gives an extraordinary interest and freshness to what he says. He shows us the meaning of sculpture as an expression of life - of human history - a thing not of galleries or museums but of the common life of the people".

A like commentary comes from the Director of the Cleveland Museum of Art, who wrote to Alec: "We had a feeling after your last talk that you had taken us into the shops of your sculptor friends in ancient Egypt and medieval Europe, showing us the essentials of your craft". And again, a comment in the bulletin of a Mid-West American college: "Those who have met (Alec Miller) already know that it is impossible to overstate what he is bringing to our students and faculty........He is an artist and scholar so good that the students break out into spontaneous applause whenever he appears".

I should add that my father lectured not only on art but frequently on literature, and was happy to tackle such subjects as Browning and Tennyson, Clough and Arnold, Scottish poetry and Ballads and much more, generally ending by reciting at length selections from any poet, for he had a fabulous Highland memory out of which he could draw whatever was asked for - including some comic delights such as Gilbert's *Bab Ballads* or *The Ingoldsby Legends*. He also had in his repertoire a good lecture on Campden and its history.

Clearly, then, immediacy was the secret of Alec's success as a speaker - being able, as Maude Royden says, to convey through his identity as 'man at the bench' the meaning of sculpture in the common life of the people of any age, including the present.

Such a faculty is always rare, so I am struck by the recollection that a comparable dedication to indivisible experience was to be found in another Cotswold artist in the '30s.[16] Michael Cardew of Winchcombe Pottery lived, as I believe my father did, in some kind of inspired relationship with his own skills and with the materials and history of his own craft. He too struggled with the matter of payment for what is fundamentally unpriceable - artistic workmanship. He too had a family to support and apprentices to pay - and, I realise as I write, he too went abroad from England. In the '30s Michael priced his pots by the weight of the clay in them with some allowance for other overheads regardless of whether he was selling a masterpiece, as some of his creations undoubtedly were, or simply a useful mug or dish. Similarly, Alec I believe had set out with the formula for price of a portrait or statue as the cost of material plus time at the bench. Such a tradesman's approach left these two free, in a way: it also left inspired work unaccounted for.

There could be other solutions, I feel, to the problem of financial recompense for the unpriceable without recourse to monopolising patronage or to the exploitative world of the middleman which all too often includes the monetary concept of 'all that the trafffic will bear'. But we seem singularly unable to come up with such a solution - and, as I tried to say earlier, the insolubility has to be lived out by creative people as best they may, which frequently means with pain and sometimes with disaster. My father was fortunate in that he maintained equilibrium in this matter both in the Old World and in the New.

It is good to know that young students, and teachers too, responded with enthusiasm to presentations and lectures along uncompromisingly work-centred lines and were more than willing to learn 'History as workmen made it'. Theses such as these were most suspect, I think, to professional connoisseurs and critics and to the art theorists. Alec Miller couldn't be pigeon-holed, and to those not particularly taken with his work he tended to say "Well, come to the bench and learn to do it better!" One or two critics embarked on written exchanges with him and one theorist, Stanley Casson, took him at his word. Casson had ideas about the tools and techniques used by the early Greek sculptors - ideas which my father knew empirically to be erroneous and unworkable. He told Casson so, and invited him to come to Campden to try working marble and stone using the techniques he was theorising about. Casson, to his credit, accepted the invitation. It was the start of a friendship valuable to both - yet I recall that Casson was never able to bring himself to work without gloves on, a fact about which I, then a brash, opinionated teen-ager, was extremely scornful. I expect my father was more tolerant: certainly he was less vocal.

The 1930s were rich in portrait assignments, and Alec also created several statuettes during those years, including the delicate and dynamic *Atalanta*. Begun at St. Nicholas at Wade and finished at Campden, she was exhibited at the Royal Academy and eventually crossed the Atlantic to be acquired by the Cleveland Museum of Art.

The *Illustrated London News* for December 12, 1931, has an interesting article by Lady Clark on Campden and its craftsmen. She has some perceptive things to say about Alec Miller: "...........His character study goes far below the surface...........with child subjects he is extraordinarily happy........his insight does not permit him to undervalue a child, or to present it merely as beauty. And this, and the irresistible attraction of everything else he does, is why they have called him over to America so many times. Psychological vision irradiates Mr. Miller's work, whether the medium be stone or the gracious wood that he loves best of all........." The article mentions, in addition to the blacksmiths, silversmiths and Paul Woodroffe's stained glass studio, The Kingsley Weavers. Owned by Leo and Eileen Baker, the Weavers had moved into the Studio after we left it. The article includes a good picture showing the big main room full of looms.

In March 1935 Alec was working on a statuette called *The Listener* when a reporter from the Birmingham Evening Dispatch happened in and decided to interview him. The result, headed "CHIPPING CAMPDEN GENIUS", is almost as fulsome and nonsensical as that of the Cleveland journalist some ten years earlier. "..........The man in the blue smock was Alec Miller, J.P., and for thirty years he has lived in Chipping Campden. For forty years he has snatched beauty out of solid, uncompromising blocks of wood. For the last twelve years he has contributed to the Academy and the statuette [*The Listener*] is to be submitted this year. It is a novel experience to watch an artist - an artist of world-wide fame, moreover - at work..........The central figure in this room which has seen the genesis of so much that has beautified the world [is] a small man with white hair and a blue smock, and cheeks the colour of Cotswold apples and a bow tie oddly at variance with the ease of the rest of his dress..........and a burr in his speech which you could never reconcile with the Cotswold dialect. Nor should you. Mr. Miller was born in Glasgow. [He] is at present engaged on work for a war memorial in Rochester, U.S.A."

And so on!

I think it was about two years later, some time in 1937, that Alec made his first trip to the Western United States, going overland and lecturing as he went. Though he knew New England and the Eastern states well and had many friends there, this was the first venture to the West coast. If I remember rightly, my mother and brother joined him there and it was on this trip that they renewed contact with the Rolfes who were living in California and with their daughter Olivia who twenty-five years earlier had played with Alec in Campden in *The Fair Maid of the West*, and her husband, geologist Harry Johnson. The Millers found California indeed a halcyon land of great appeal, freedom and friendliness, exemplified especially by the Johnson milieu of informal hospitality, much knowledge of the region and much interesting company. To my father it was a great pleasure to get together with Professor Rolfe, who had so many years before organised lecture tours in the United States for C.R.Ashbee.

It was a more than congenial visit for both Alec and Eleanor Miller. Rolfes and Johnsons were persuasive, offers of work had abounded, and I believe my parents returned to Campden with strong promptings to uproot themselves from England entirely and opt for the expansive West. The threat of another war was surely included in their thinking, and the impulse to move was made more specific by the marriage of Alistair to a Westerner and the prospect of his settling in California.

Though I know my father's feelings, and my mother's too, were positive about the adventure, I am sure that leaving Campden must have been quite a traumatic undertaking for them both. Their confidence in what they were doing was certainly well founded: my father never lacked for work, even in the war years. He was still executing carving and lecturing commissions in his eighties, when living in Santa Barbara, in addition to doing much writing.

His book, *Stone and Marble Carving*, was published in 1948, both in England and in the U.S., and *Tradition in Sculpture* followed in 1949. Both these books were big undertakings. For the stone and marble carving treatise, Alec carved a portrait of a child in marble, photographing the work at every stage from the preliminary measurements through the hazards of carving to the final saw-cut by which the bust was made ready for its wood base. In the same way, the carving of a portrait relief in stone and of a 3-foot draped statue was carefully documented and photographed and the same done for lettering on stone.

The dedicated practicality of the book makes fascinating reading, "In this simple, lucid manual of workshop practice lies the funded knowledge of more than forty years of work" wrote Lewis Mumford in his preface to the American edition. A perceptive review (written by his son-in-law for a California paper) says: "These sane and lively chapters are utterly free of abstract persiflage. Their importance lies very largely in their simplicity. If they constitute a very considerable statement about art that is because they do so much to unite art with work, and if Mr. Miller writes as a master craftsman that is because he has also always remained in the position of the student and the disciple."

The book has a dedication "To the stonemasons of Oxford, who for more than a quarter of a century have helped me to appreciate the 'mystery' of their craft: particularly to three - Harry Fathers, Tom Groves and Tom Barrett, to the wisdom of whose hands I have so often been indebted".

Sadly, both these books are currently out of print.

My parents returned to England and Campden on visits several times in the 40s and 50s, and during those years my father wrote his account called *C.R.Ashbee and the Guild of Handicraft*. It remains unpublished, but has been drawn upon by Fiona McCarthy for her book *The Simple Life* and by Alan Crawford for his tremendous work on Ashbee.

The last meeting between Alec Miller and Charlie Downer outside the Guild House, 1961. Both men died later that year.

It was, I think, particularly to meet again with Janet Ashbee that my parents made a trip to England in 1961, although my father's health was not good. They were staying at St. Nicholas at Wade and expecting to go North and visit Janet at Hest Bank, when news came of her death. The blow to my father was a mortal one - and yet like all such it opened a door, this time to his own release. He died on May 17th, CRA's birthday and the day Janet's ashes were laid to rest. After the funeral conducted by his nephew John Bishop in St. Nicholas church where he had been married fifty-two years before, Alec was buried in the village cemetery, close to the grave of his brother-in-law and friend, Arthur Bernhard Smith. My mother and brother had been with him, though I was far away, and - such are the workings of Providence - among those following the cart to the cemetary were Olivia and Harry Johnson, cosmopolitans who perhaps embodied Alec's most meaningful and affectionate link with the New World.

Letters came to my mother from all directions, and many from Campden. Harry Warmington wrote: "Alec will always be remembered by all at the Guild for his many kindnesses and unfailing good humour: his death came as a great shock to us all, particularly to Charlie Downer. For the first time he suddenly seemed to feel his 84 years......."

'Pam' Mairet wrote: "My first meeting with Alec, very nearly 55 years ago, was in the passage at the top of the stairs in Braithwaite House. I can see him now, in the candlelight with his shorts and bare knees, giving a welcome-reception to me, the callow young stranger, and helping me with my trunk......I quickly discovered that he was the most loved of all in that memorable community of young men".

To see the man as 'Pam' remembered him is to see truly. Christopher Morley, American writer and long-time friend, also has something very true to say in an appreciation of Alec Miller's carvings, written in the long-ago 20s. "They have a little message all their own, I keep thinking: here in the actual traces of the sculptor's chisel we are face to face with the Task itself. No intermediate process stands between our eyes and the artist's work......Surely even the most untutored of us - such as this uncertificated volunteer - can enjoy, and learn profitable humility from, an art so unpretending, so lovely, so patiently frugal and true".

Indeed we can! And those are splendid adjectives, evoking as they do the work and this particular worker: the man at the bench, and especially the man at the bench in Campden.

ON SOURCES

This small-scale memoir does little more than give an informal glimpse of Alec Miller's life and work. Much in-depth study remains to be done before the full range of his cultural contribution can be worthily assessed and presented.

My sources have been largely my father's own writings. He left more than one account of his Glasgow childhood and youth. The few letters that have survived were of great help in attempting to convey his life and thought during the period of his transition from employed Guildsman to independent craftsman. His unpublished *C.R.Ashbee and the Guild of Handicraft* was also a rich source of information and colour.

I record a great debt to Fiona MacCarthy's lively book, *The Simple Life* and to Alan Crawford's monumental *C.R.Ashbee*. Both these books are enormously rewarding reading for anyone seeking a full account of the Guild of Handicraft and its impact on Campden - and on the world at large.

J.W.

TEXTUAL NOTES

p.11, No.1   Crawford, Alan: *C.R. Ashbee. Architect, Designer and Romantic Socialist* Yale University Press. 1985

p.11, No. 2   Osborn, Harry T.: *A Child in Arcadia.* Campden & District Historical and Archaeological Society, (2nd Edition) 1997.

p.12, No.3   The Lichfield Cross. This is still in general use on the High Altar of the Cathedral. It is described as follows:- Silver with some gilding and blue enamel enrichments, with mother-of-pearl and moonstones in symbolic vine. Angels round the "bar of heaven" with gilded halos and enamelled wings: m o t h e r - o f - p e a r l matrix, emblematic of the Blessed Virgin Mary surmounted by the figure of St. Chad. (The Cathedral is dedicated to Saint Mary and St.Chad): the tripod base suggested by the candlesticks. Designed by Mr. Ashbee. Made by the Guild of Handicrafts. Given by Miss S. Lonsdale as a Thankoffering. Dedicated Christmas Eve 1906. 45.5 inches high.

p.15, No.4   MacCarthy,Fiona: *The Simple Life - C.R.Ashbee in the Cotswolds.* Lund Humphries, London (1981)

p.15, No.5   Cecil Brewer. London architect of the firm of Smith and Brewer, friend and associate of C.R.Ashbee. Designed Mary Ward Building, Tavistock Place WC1 with A. Dunbar Smith, and Heal's shop, Tottenham Court Road.

p17, No.6   MacCarthy, Fiona - see 4 above

p.20, No.7   Frederick L. Griggs, master etcher, long -time Campden inhabitant, enthusiast and benefactor. Griggses and Millers were close friends, especially in the early years.

p.21, No.8   Philippe A. Mairet, familiarly known as 'Pam'. A gifted actor, writer and later editor. Pam came to Campden as a student of architecture under Ashbee. He and Millers became lifelong friends.

p.25, No.9   Wentworth Huyshe, scholar and medievalist. Huyshe participated in Guild plays, and became a well-known Campden character.

p.37, No.10   'Teapot' mentioned on p.33 and pp.68 & 69 of *A Child in Arcadia* H.T.Osborn (see above). James 'Teapot' Williams was one of Campden's best known characters, living in Sheep Street. He did odd jobs like bird-scaring.

p.37, No.11   Bob Dickinson also mentioned in *A Child in Arcadia* pps.51-52,54-55,73 and 74. He sold the News of the World and lived in Cider Mill Lane. Mr. Osborn tells the story of his encounter with King Edward VII to whom he sold a copy of the newspaper.

p.38, No.12   Scuttlebrook Wake. A local fair, held on the Saturday in Whit week each year. Stalls and Sideshows are set up in Leysbourne, where the Scuttle Brook used to flow (it is now piped underground). It is preceded by a fancy dress procession and the Crowning of the Scuttlebrook Queen, who opens the Fair. The Dover's Games are held on the preceding evening on Dover's Hill.

p.38, No.13   Old Campden House.The ruins of the fine seventeenth century mansion, with its two elegant Banqueting Houses and twin Gatehouses built next to the Parish Church by Baptist Hicks, Lord Campden, and burnt down in the Civil Wars.

p.38, No.14   Mr. Pyment. James W.Pyment (see *A Child in Arcadia* pp.11,14,39,59,61) foreman of the cabinet-makers in the Guild of Handicraft. He moved to Campden from London with C.R.Ashbee and the Guild, and settled in the town,forming his own company of builders and woodworkers, with its headquarters in the Silk Mill after the Guild collapsed.

p.59, No.15   Quoted from Raines, John & Day-Lower, Donna: *Modern Work and Human Meaning*. Westminster Press, USA (1986).

p.61, No.16   George Hart might be considered another. However, the special considerations which attend workers in precious metals and precious stones put them in a category different from those in the less recondite crafts - or so it seems to me.

INDEX

ALEC MILLER